FLYING ACES OF WORLD WAR I

WORLD Landmark BOOKS

RANDOM HOUSE   NEW YORK

FLYING ACES OF WORLD WAR I

by Gene Gurney

Illustrated with photographs

All photographs in this book are from the United States Air Force with the exception of the following: Bettmann Archive, pp. 4, 12, 27, 37 (top), 59; Lt. Col. Kimbrough S. Brown, pp. 20, 62, 121, 127; Culver Pictures, pp. 7 (left), 25, 30, 56; The Daily News, p. 146; European Picture Service, p. 17; The Granger Collection, p. 7 (right); Imperial War Museum, pp. 71, 74, 76, 105, 118; National Archives/Army Air Forces, pp. 45, 110, 161; National Archives/U. S. Navy, pp. 133, 135, National Archives/U. S. Signal Corps, p. 115; Robert Soubiran (through USAF), title page, pp. 37 (bottom), 95, 119; United Press International, p. 109.

Cover Painting: Francis A. Chauncy

To Clare

CONTENTS

FLYING ACES OF WORLD WAR I

THE AIRPLANE GOES TO WAR

The immediate cause of World War I was an assassin's bullets. The fateful shots were fired in Sarajevo, the capital of the Austro-Hungarian province of Bosnia, on June 28, 1914. On that day the heir to the throne of Austria-Hungary, Francis Ferdinand, who was in Sarajevo to observe the summer maneuvers of the Austrian army, went for a ride through the city in an open motor car. His consort, the Duchess of Hohenberg, accompanied him. As the couple traveled through the sunlit streets of Sarajevo, a young man named Gavrilo Princip quietly joined a group of people who were waiting for a glimpse of the Archduke. When the royal entourage approached the spot where Princip stood, the young Bosnian stepped forward, aimed a pistol at the Archduke, and fired.

At the sound of the shots the horses in the procession neighed and reared in fright. The Archduke

Archduke Francis Ferdinand with his wife approximately one hour before their assassination.

grasped his throat and fell forward; the Duchess collapsed against him. In an instant the soldiers accompanying Francis Ferdinand had wheeled their mounts and surrounded Princip. It was too late to do anything for the Archduke. Both he and his consort had been fatally wounded.

Why did Gavrilo Princip shoot the man who someday would have been the ruler of the great Austro-Hungarian Empire? The reason was political. Like many of his fellow Bosnians, Princip wanted his country to be independent. "Why should we be ruled by officials in faraway Vienna?" he asked.

To carry on their fight for independence, Bosnians had organized a number of secret societies. After Princip's arrest, it was discovered that he belonged to one of them, the Black Hand. It was also discovered that the members of the Black Hand had received weapons and training from Serbia, Bosnia's neighbor on the east.

Serbia had long been interested in Bosnia because of the many Serbians living in that country. When secret societies were organized in Bosnia to fight for self-government, Serbia did what she could to help them. In some cases high officials of the Serbian army worked with members of Bosnian groups like the Black Hand.

When Gavrilo Princip's connection with the Black Hand and with Serbia became known, the Austro-Hungarian government decided that something had to be done to end Serbia's meddling. The assassination of the Archduke called for more than a mere protest to Serbia.

First, Austria went to her powerful ally, Germany. Would Kaiser Wilhelm back Austria in any action she might take against Serbia? Both countries, along with Italy, were members of a defensive treaty organization known as the Triple Alliance. The three nations had agreed to support one another in case of attack by two or more great powers.

On July 5 the German emperor promised Austria his support. Austria then prepared a message which was presented to Serbia on July 23. It contained a series of demands: Serbia must ban all anti-Austrian publications and societies, dismiss anti-Austrian officials, and permit Austria to continue her investigation of the assassination within Serbia itself. Serbia had just forty-eight hours in which to answer.

Before the time expired, Serbia agreed to most of Austria's requests and offered to submit the others to an international court. But at the same time she mobilized her army.

Austria decided that Serbia's reply was unsatisfactory, and on July 28 she declared war on the small Balkan country.

To the east, Serbia's friend and protector, Russia, had been watching the growing crisis. On July 29 she ordered a partial mobilization of troops on her southern border, then cancelled the order, only to reinstate it the next day.

Germany, too, had been keeping a close check on developments. When the worried Russians ordered a general mobilization on July 31, Germany issued an ultimatum demanding that the troops be sent home within twelve hours. Russia did not reply, and by noon on August 1 the two countries were at war.

Russia, too, belonged to an alliance. With her partners, France and England, she had formed the Triple Entente. Because of the alliance between Russia and France, Germany began to move troops toward the west as well as toward the east and formally declared

Kaiser Wilhelm II   *Alfred von Schlieffen*

war on France on August 3, 1914.

For many years German generals had feared they might someday have to fight Russia and France at the same time. No country wants to fight a two-front war. To avoid such a situation a great German general, Alfred von Schlieffen, had worked out a very clever plan. He proposed that the German army deal with France first. "In six weeks of intensive fighting," said Schlieffen, "France can be conquered leaving the German army free to concentrate its entire attention on Russia."

The success of Schlieffen's plan depended upon the speed with which the German army could move into France. Germany and France had many miles of border in common, but the most direct route was not the fastest. Mountains and rough terrain made much of the border difficult to cross, and strong forts protected the areas where troops might attempt to pass.

Another way to reach France from Germany was through Belgium and Holland. General von Schlieffen chose that route. He proposed to send the German army through Belgium and Holland to the English Channel, down into the heart of France, then eastward back toward Germany. The French army, retreating before the German onslaught, would be crushed against a second German force waiting in eastern France.

Schlieffen died before the war began, but his successor, General Helmuth von Moltke, followed part of his strategy for getting into France. He sent the German armies through Belgium, flouting Belgian neutrality. The invasion of neutral Belgium brought another country into the war—England.

In addition to being an ally of France and Russia, England had promised to come to the aid of Belgium. To fulfill her obligations and to protect herself from the growing threat across the Channel, England declared war on Germany on August 4. The shots fired at Sarajevo had now plunged the most powerful countries of Europe into a great and deadly war.

The conflict continued to spread. Japan, honoring a treaty with England, entered the war against Germany in August. In October Turkey joined the Central Powers (Germany and Austria–Hungary). Italy at first declared herself neutral. She had always been an unenthusiastic member of the Triple Alliance because she regarded Austria as more of an enemy than a friend. Finally, in 1915, Italy joined the Western Allies, and many of the Balkan countries eventually did likewise. In 1917 the United States and other countries of the Western Hemisphere entered the conflict on the side of England and France. By the time the war ended, more than forty countries were involved. But before that day arrived many bloody battles had to be fought.

The initial German drive toward the west worked as General von Schlieffen had predicted. While England hurriedly sent soldiers and supplies to help her allies, the German armies overran Belgium and entered France. Then General von Moltke decided he could defeat the French more quickly if he changed Schlieffen's plan. He would speed things up by attacking France at once along her eastern border. Instead of waiting until the main German force had swept across France from the west, von Moltke ordered an immediate offensive in the east. And he ordered his forces to pass northeast of Paris

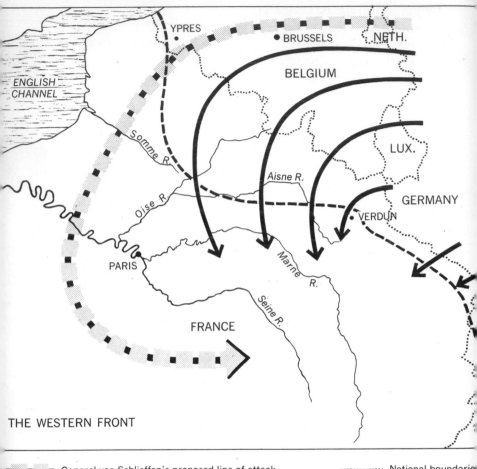

THE WESTERN FRONT

■ ■ ■ General von Schlieffen's proposed line of attack

━━━ General von Moltke's actual attack routes

•••••••• National boundaries

━ ━ ━ Trench battleline established during the early stages of World War I

Map labels: YPRES, BRUSSELS, NETH., ENGLISH CHANNEL, BELGIUM, Somme R., LUX., Oise R., Aisne R., GERMANY, VERDUN, PARIS, Marne R., Seine R., FRANCE instead of going around the city in a wide circle to the south.

The fortifications along France's eastern border, especially at Verdun, proved too strong for the German offensive. At Paris, von Moltke ran into more trouble as French and English forces moved up to meet the enemy. In a four-day battle, fought between September 6 and 9 near the Marne River, the Allies were able to stop the German advance. The Battle of the Marne was the first great turning point of the war.

The German armies were forced to retreat to the Aisne River. From their stand on the Aisne they tried to move northward around the Allied armies. The Allies in turn tried to move around the Germans, but neither side could outflank the other. By winter the two forces had fought their way to the North Sea and the battleline stretched from there to the Swiss border.

While she fought against France and England on the Western Front, Germany was also fighting Russia on the Eastern Front. In this area Germany received some help from her ally, Austria-Hungary. But it was Germany that gave Russia her first big defeat. The Russians attempted to invade German East Prussia in August and at Tannenberg lost almost an entire army.

Germany won no victories like Tannenberg on the Western Front. After November neither side was

British infantry in front-line trenches prepare for the zero hour.

strong enough to advance. Unable to move forward, both the Germans and the Allies dug trenches while they sought a way out of the stalemate. They brought in barbed wire to protect their trench barriers. Behind the trenches they installed artillery and built flying fields. From the flying fields airmen took off to check on the enemy. Traveling back and forth above the battlelines, they spotted targets for the guns of the artillerymen and watched for enemy troop movements that could mean an attack was about to begin.

In 1914 military leaders were by no means agreed

on what use should be made of aircraft in fighting a war. Some of them thought the flying "bird cages" should not be used at all, for this was still the day of the cavalryman who went to war on horseback. The noisy flying machines might frighten the horses.

But military authorities did agree that success on the battlefield depended in part on knowledge of the enemy's movements. In the past, observers in balloons had been able to gather useful information. But because of greater freedom of movement, observers in airplanes were able to cover more territory, including areas behind the enemy's lines.

So the airplane was used chiefly for observation during the first months of the war, although a few pilots did experiment with dropping bombs on the enemy. The first "bomber" may have been Ferdinand von Hiddessen's Aviatik biplane from which the German pilot dropped bombs on Paris in August of 1914. He flew over the city one night at five o'clock and dropped three 6-pound bombs, all his plane could carry. Since the bombs were simply tossed overboard, they did very little damage, but the concept of aerial bombing was to grow in importance.

All the warring countries had airplanes in 1914, but many of them were not suitable for reconnaissance. Observation of the enemy called for a slow, stable craft that would give the pilot, and the observer who sometimes rode with him, a good chance to look around. A camera was considered necessary equipment but a gun was not. Soldiers on the ground could take care of the shooting. In fact enemy pilots, if they weren't too busy at the controls, were apt to pass by with a friendly wave.

Before long, however, the observers began to fill their pockets with objects to toss at enemy aircraft. Half-bricks were said to be a favorite weapon. Or sometimes the men would fling a length of chain through the air. Such measures caused little damage— even after pistols replaced the bricks and chains.

But when rifles began to replace the pistols, the aerial shooting became serious. Only the difficulty of loading and aiming a rifle within the narrow confines of the cockpit kept the weapon from becoming much more deadly. The observer acted as the gunner, and he had to shoot at a moving target through a maze of wires, struts, and whirling propeller blades. Instead of hitting the enemy, he often hit parts of his own plane.

The next step was the airborne machine gun. A British pilot, Lieutenant Louis A. Strange, and his observer, Lieutenant Penn Gaskell, took the first one into the air. They had "borrowed" it from their squadron storeroom. It was a Lewis machine gun and very heavy. In fact it was so heavy Strange could climb no higher than 3,500 feet. The German plane he hoped to catch was cruising around at an altitude of 5,000 feet. Gaskell, however, did manage to fire the gun, producing a great deal of noise and vibration but no effect at all on the enemy.

The development of more powerful airplanes helped to solve the problem of lifting a heavy machine gun into the air. But there remained the even greater problem of locating a gun where a pilot or observer could reach it, aim, and fire without hitting his own airplane. On some planes machine guns were located on brackets that raised them above the whirling propeller. In that position a gun could be fired without too much trouble, but it was impossible to load additional ammunition or to make repairs during a flight. Another experiment placed a machine gun just outside the cockpit, next to the pilot. That worked too, but the pilot had to fly sideways into the target in order to aim his gun.

Military aviators in every country worked on the problem of using a machine gun in the air. One of them was Roland Garros, who became the first real combat pilot of World War I.

Garros had already won fame as a flier when he joined one of the first observation squadrons to be organized by the French. A former student of the piano, Garros had originally gone to Paris to complete his musical education. There he saw his first airplane and before long the piano was forgotten. Garros persuaded the famous Brazilian airplane designer, Alberto Santos-Dumont, to teach him to fly. He proved an apt pupil; soon he was one of the best fliers in France. Garros took part in air races and made exhibition flights in Europe and in the United States. In 1913 he became the first man to fly across the Mediterranean Sea. The 453-mile trip from southern France to Tunisia took him a little less than eight hours.

On the day war was declared Garros was in Germany, where he had been giving exhibition flights. As a French citizen he faced arrest as an enemy alien. Fortunately, in the excitement caused by the war declaration, neither Garros nor his plane was closely guarded. He was able to take off that night and fly back to France. (Very few people had ever attempted to fly at night.) In addition, he managed to take off without the help of the several Germans who had made up his ground crew.

On his return to Paris, Garros reported for military service. Soon he was flying above the advancing German army, checking on its strength and location. And he began to think about ways of using a gun in the air. He felt that a pilot should be able to reach his gun easily and fire it directly forward. In other words, he should be able to aim his plane at the enemy and shoot.

But what about the propeller? Garros had heard that a French flier named Eugene Gilbert had tried wrapping the propeller blades with steel-wire tape to deflect the bullets that struck them. While Gilbert was experimenting with this idea, ricocheting bullets

Reporters interview Roland Garros (center) after one of his prewar flights.

killed two men who were helping him. So the project was abandoned.

Garros figured that less than seven percent of the bullets he fired would strike the propeller. To guard against accidents from that seven percent, he designed triangular metal shields for the back of the propeller blades. The shields were angled to deflect bullets away from the plane and the pilot.

Garros started work on his forward-firing gun in February, 1915. On April 1 he was ready to take such a gun, mounted behind the propeller and fitted with steel deflector pieces, into the air against the enemy. He flew a French Morane-Saulnier biplane, since his regular Morane-Saulnier monoplane was not in working order that day.

Soon after take-off, Garros spotted four German two-place Albatros observation planes heading for the French lines. He caught up with them, turned into the nearest one, and fired. A burst of machine-gun bullets flew through his whirling propeller, and the Albatros went down. Garros ended his pass in a dive but he quickly regained altitude. Once more, flames sparkled brightly between his propeller blades; a second Albatros exploded in midair. The two surviving Albatros pilots headed for home at full throttle.

For the next two weeks Roland Garros flew his Morane over the battleground. His forward-firing gun shot down five German planes, and he became the first Allied ace of World War I.

At that time "ace" was a word applied to anyone who accomplished something outstanding. The man who won a bicycle race was an ace. So was the soldier who performed an act of special bravery. But when the newspapers began to carry numerous stories about "that ace among pilots, Roland Garros," and the planes he had downed, the word acquired a new meaning. An ace was a pilot who shot down five planes.

Garros and his Morane caused considerable consternation among German pilots and observers. Those who saw him in action reported: "He seems to be firing between the blades of his propeller, but that is impossible."

Impossible or not, Garros' bullets were finding their mark. German pilots became very cautious about flying where they might meet up with the deadly French monoplane. Then on April 19 engine trouble forced Garros down behind the German lines. Pilots on both sides were under instructions to burn their planes if they came down in enemy territory. It was especially important that the Morane be destroyed because of the secret shield on the propeller. If the Germans learned about it, they too could fire a gun through propeller blades.

The Morane wouldn't burn. The plane was wet and nothing the frantic Garros could do would set it afire. The French flier was taken prisoner, but his plane received more attention from his captors than he did. It was taken to Berlin where Anthony Fokker, a Dutch airplane designer working in Germany, was asked to take a look at the shield on the propeller blades.

"We would like you to work out something like this for our planes," the German generals told Fokker.

Anthony Fokker, who had a quick, scientific mind, realized at once that he must try to do more than copy Garros' idea. Even with improved protection for the blades, the Morane propeller was bound to shatter sooner or later under the impact of a steady stream of bullets. But Fokker thought there must be a mathematical solution to the problem. If the two blades of the propeller passed before the gun 2,400 times a minute and the gun fired 600 times a minute, it should be possible to figure out a way to fire the gun only when there was no propeller blade in the way.

What Fokker did was to work out a mechanism that would prevent the gun from firing when the propeller was in the way. The trigger was released

Anthony Fokker loads two Spandau machine guns for a test firing against the synchronization mechanism of a Fokker Dreidecker. The wings have not yet been installed.

during the time a blade passed in front of the gun. By the time the weapon fired, the propeller blade was no longer in front of the gun. Within forty-eight hours Fokker's interrupter device had been made to work on the ground. Next he successfully used it in one of his Eindeckers (monoplanes). In less than a month Eindeckers equipped with the new device were shooting French and British planes out of the sky.

The day of the friendly wave from an enemy pilot was gone forever. Now a shooting war was being fought in the air as well as on the ground. Increasing numbers of observation planes and bombers roamed over the battlefields. Armed single-seater planes known as pursuits or scouts—today they would be called fighters—were used to drive them off. Flying a single-seater required a special kind of skill and daring. The best of these pilots won fame as the flying aces of World War I.

GEORGES GUYNEMER OF THE STORKS

While Roland Garros worked out the details of his plan to fire a gun through the propeller blades of his Morane, another young Frenchman made his first solo flight at an aviation school in Pau in the southwestern part of France. His name was Georges Guynemer, and he became one of the most famous air heroes of World War I.

When the war began, Guynemer was nineteen years old. Like many of his compatriots he reported at once for army duty. In 1914 the French army required its enlistees to pass a physical examination. The doctor who examined Guynemer shook his head. "You are too thin, too frail," he said. "Go home and build yourself up." In the terminology of the French army, Guynemer had been "postponed."

The unhappy Guynemer had often been ill as a child. Constant colds and a weak stomach kept him from gaining weight and strength. His delicate, almost girlish, features made him appear even more frail than he actually was.

What Guynemer lacked in strength he made up in determination. He returned to the enlistment center with his father, a retired army officer. But even the elder Guynemer couldn't convince the doctors that his son was strong enough to make a good soldier. Once again the verdict was—"postponed."

Guynemer refused to give up; there must be some way he could help his country. He went next to the big aviation camp at Pau. "I will do anything, anything at all, if only you will take me," he told the commandant.

The *Aviation Militaire,* as the French called their air service, needed more men. In the first months of the war there weren't enough pilots to fly the planes or enough mechanics to keep them repaired. Young Guynemer didn't look strong, but he seemed to be an intelligent and determined youth. In addition he had studied engineering. The commandant decided to give the eager young man a chance. He told Guynemer he would try him as a student mechanic.

The life of a student, or apprentice, mechanic was a hard one even for a strong, healthy young man. The apprentices were expected to do all the heaviest and dirtiest jobs. They spent long hours cleaning and repairing engines. Every day they had to move heavy cans of gas and oil. Guynemer did his share without complaining—even when his fellow mechanics called him "Mademoiselle" and gave him the dirtiest engines to clean.

Whenever he could Guynemer watched the expert mechanics repair wings and other damaged airplane parts. In this way he learned a great deal about how an airplane worked. Soon he had a new ambition: to learn to fly. He began to spend his spare time on the flight line.

One of the pilots at Pau later wrote of Guynemer: "I had already had my attention drawn to this 'little girl' dressed in a private's uniform whom one met in the camp, his hands covered with castor oil, his face all stains, his clothes torn. I did not know what he did in the workshop, but he certainly did not add to its brilliance by his appearance. We saw him at all times hanging around the planes. His highly interested little face amused us. When we landed he watched us with such admiration and envy! He asked us endless questions and constantly wanted explanations. Without seeming to do so he was learning. For a reply to some question about the art of flying, he would run to the other end of the camp to get gasoline for our tanks."

Guynemer knew that from time to time a few student mechanics were transferred to pilot training. He wrote home to his father. Could any of the elder Guynemer's army friends help arrange such a transfer? One of them could and did. In January, 1915, a new list of student pilots was posted and Georges Guynemer's name was on it.

Guynemer proved an apt pupil. His first plane was a Blériot *rolleur*. The Blériot, like many French planes had been named after its designer. A *rolleur* did not leave the ground. The students called it the Penguin because of its abbreviated wings. In the Penguin they taxied up and down the airfield, learning how to handle the engine and controls while they

Georges Guynemer

were still safely on the ground. Then came a Blériot with enough power to get as high as 150 feet into the air.

After a little more than a month as a student pilot, Guynemer soloed in a fully powered plane. Early in June he was graduated and sent to *Escadrille M.S. 3*. *Escadrille* is the French word for squadron. The initials *M.S.* refer to the plane flown by the escadrille —the Morane-Saulnier.

Escadrille M.S. 3 would later become one of the five famous *Cigogne,* or Stork, Squadrons. These squadrons were made up of men who had become aces —the best fliers of the *Aviation Militaire.* Each one of their planes carried a picture of a stork on its side. When Georges Guynemer joined M.S. 3, some of the pilots who were to become the heroes of France were already members of the squadron.

Early in the war France began to divide her air force into three main branches. One branch was to take care of reconnaissance work; that is, it was to collect information on where the enemy was located and what he was doing. Another was to concentrate on dropping bombs on the enemy. The third branch was to fight the enemy in the air. M.S. 3 was slated to become a squadron of fighters, whose pilots would fly in speedy, single-seater planes. When Guynemer reported for duty, however, the squadron was flying reconnaissance patrols in two-seater Morane-Saulniers. An observer rode in the seat behind the pilot to locate

Drawing of a two-seater reconnaissance plane in which the observer is mapping the position of the enemy.

enemy troops and enemy guns. He also took pictures with his camera and drew maps of the country over which he flew.

Guynemer's first two patrols as a member of M.S. 3 were uneventful. On his third trip over the German lines his plane was hit by gunfire from the ground.

The Morane shuddered under the impact of the shells, flipped over, and righted itself. A startled Guynemer cautiously tested the controls. Then he put the nose down and headed for home. His first combat experience had been a close call. He was glad he was still alive.

As he flew along he examined the Morane. It seemed to be flying all right. Evidently the damage was not serious. Guynemer knew that his observer hadn't finished his reconnaissance. Should they go back? Because the noise of the engine and the distance between the two men made it difficult for them to hear one another, they had to communicate with signs. But the observer indicated that he was willing to return if Guynemer wanted to. So back they flew toward the German guns that had already hit them once. Guynemer circled until the observer had completed his assignment, which included a sketch of the enemy gun emplacements. Then they went home.

That was the beginning of Guynemer's reputation as a cool and fearless flier. His fellow pilots in Escadrille M.S. 3 had been disappointed when they first saw the frail newcomer. He hadn't looked as if he would be capable of flying an airplane at all, certainly not in combat. But now they began to think they might have been wrong about him.

On July 19, 1915, Guynemer flew on another patrol. Once again he had an observer riding with him, a man named Guerder. They spotted two German planes and turned to pursue the nearer one. Guerder had a machine gun in the rear cockpit. It was on a rigid mount and could not be swung around to follow the movements of the enemy plane. Instead Guynemer had to maneuver his plane so that the gun would be pointed in the right direction.

While he was trying to get into the right position, the second German plane moved in. The observer riding in the enemy craft fired at Guynemer and Guerder with a rifle. Georges was able to bank away and Guerder's machine gun went into action. The German ship went down in flames.

Because both pilot and observer had done their jobs well, each was credited with an aerial victory. For Georges Guynemer it was the first of the fifty-three officially credited victories that were to make him France's second-ranking ace.

In September, 1915, new single-seater Nieuport fighters were delivered to Escadrille M.S. 3. The unit's designation then became N. 3. The members of the escadrille painted a picture of a stork on the side of each of the new planes. Because of this they soon gained fame as *Les Cigognes,* or the Storks.

The French air service had not adopted Roland Garros' plan for firing a gun through a plane's propeller. The scheme was too dangerous. Instead the Nieuports of 1915 carried a Lewis machine gun on the top wing. In that position the gun fired above the arc of the propeller.

Guynemer displays two machine guns taken from the plane of one of his victims.

Early in December, 1915, Georges Guynemer scored his first victory in one of the new planes. He was flying alone over German territory, however, so no one saw the enemy aircraft go down. In order to be officially credited as a victory, the enemy machine had to come down inside the French lines. Or observers in the air or on the ground must see it go down. The rules of the *Aviation Militaire* were very strict on this point. As a result, almost every ace downed a number of planes which he could not officially add to his score. Toward the end of the war, when the Germans were falling back, the wrecks of some of these planes were discovered on what had once been German territory. These were then credited to the pilots who claimed them.

On December 8 Guynemer downed a plane that did count. Before the week was over he had two more. And he still found time to do some flying in the squadron's old Moranes. There was always a great deal of reconnaissance work to be done.

On Christmas Eve, 1915, his twenty-first birthday, Georges Guynemer received the Cross of the Legion of Honor, one of France's highest awards. The citation read: "A pilot of great gallantry, a model of devotion to duty and courage. During the course of the past two months he has fulfilled two missions of a special nature requiring the highest spirit of self-sacrifice and has engaged in thirteen aerial combats, of which two ended in the destruction in flames of the enemy aircraft."

On February 21, 1916, the German army launched a major attack against the fortifications at Verdun on the Meuse River in northeastern France. Verdun was one of the main barriers on the road to Paris from the east. The Germans hoped a breakthrough there would cause French resistance to collapse.

The attack began with nine hours of artillery fire that wiped out everything in its path. When German infantrymen advanced behind the barrage, they were met by resolute French soldiers. Both sides brought in reinforcements, and fierce battles raged every day for a week. On February 29th the exhausted Germans called a temporary halt to their attack. Although French losses had been heavy, France refused to give up Verdun.

As the fighting continued through the spring and summer, however, the French were forced into a slow retreat. Sometimes they were able to recapture a position that had been lost, only to have the Germans take it away again. Then in the fall the French launched a series of attacks that eventually turned the tide against the Germans.

Both Germany and France made extensive use of their air forces in the fight for Verdun. Georges Guynemer's unit moved to the Verdun front in March, 1916. Even though the Nieuport didn't have a machine gun that fired through the propeller, it proved to be a better airplane than the Fokker Eindecker, which the Germans were using. Enemy fliers thought twice before attacking a Nieuport.

Not long after the move to Verdun, Guynemer was wounded. The pilot of a German biplane zeroed in on the Frenchman's Nieuport before he had time to maneuver. Lead slammed through the windscreen into the cockpit. Two of the bullets lodged in Guynemer's arm, and his face and scalp were cut by pieces of the damaged windscreen.

The Nieuport went into a dangerous spin. Guynemer was barely able to see because of the blood that covered his eyes. With his uninjured arm he managed to regain control of the plane and land it at the nearest French airfield. From there he was rushed to a hospital in Paris.

After he had been in the hospital a little more than a month, Guynemer talked the doctors into releasing him. He wanted to get back to the fighting at Verdun. Although he was thinner than ever and still wore a bandage on his left arm, he was eager to fly again.

Guynemer, like most pilots who had narrowly survived an air battle, approached his next flight with a certain amount of fear. Perhaps he had lost his touch. If so, any reasonably competent German airmen would be able to hit him. The only way to find out was to fly, so Guynemer climbed into a Nieuport and took off.

The first plane that he spotted was a Rumpler, a German observation ship. The pilot had a forward-firing gun; in the rear cockpit an observer manned a second gun. This encounter would be a real test of the French pilot's skill.

Guynemer, who was flying above the Germans, circled and came down head-on into the Rumpler. For a second he held the enemy pilot in his sights, but he did not fire. By the time the startled German pressed his trigger, Guynmer had dived under the two-seater. He came around for another pass, but once more he held his fire. Then he quickly shifted position to concentrate on the observer, who was firing continuously.

During the next few minutes Guynemer gave

A captured German Rumpler.

neither enemy gunner a target he could hit. His Nieuport was like an elusive mosquito buzzing around the Rumpler. Finally Guynemer's tactics so unnerved the German pilot that he broke away and headed for home at full throttle.

Back on the ground, Guynemer explained his strange maneuvers: "I could have hit them a dozen times, but they must have fired five hundred rounds without hitting me." The French ace had not lost his touch.

By the end of July, 1916, he had destroyed a total of eleven enemy aircraft. Meanwhile, Escadrille N. 3 moved again, this time to the Somme River area, where the British army had launched an attack against the Germans. The Storks were assigned to help the airmen of Britain's Royal Flying Corps.

While battles raged in the air above the Western Front, the French aircraft industry constantly improved the military airplane. The Fokker Eindecker with its deadly forward-firing gun had been giving German pilots a distinct advantage in aerial combat. Although both England and France tried hard to develop similar firing systems for their fighter planes, neither country had an Anthony Fokker. Thus it was some months before English and French pilots had synchronized machine guns.

Then in September, 1916, the Storks received another new fighter plane, the Spad. It was one of the best of the single-seater planes developed during

World War I. And its machine gun was equipped with an interrupter device for forward firing.

Georges Guynemer was one of the first to try the new plane. He found the Spad so easy to fly and its gun so effective that he quickly doubled his score of enemy planes shot down. By the end of 1916 he had twenty-five victories to his credit, the highest score in the *Aviation Militaire*.

When the Storks moved back to northeastern France early in 1917, Guynemer's score continued to mount. He was promoted to the rank of captain and received many decorations and medals for his work in the air. The hero of all France, he remained the same hard-working pilot he had always been. His health was still frail. In fact it was worse, for he was beginning to feel the strain of two years of constant flying.

When Guynemer's score reached a total of fifty-three German planes destroyed, his commanders urged him to retire from active flying. They were concerned about his failing health. They were concerned, too, about the effect on the morale of the French people if the country's leading ace should be shot down.

But the great Guynemer seemed invincible. German bullets could hit him but they couldn't keep him out of the sky. He was shot down no fewer than seven times—once over no man's land, as the area between the battlelines was called. On that occasion French troops saw his badly damaged plane come down and

(Above) Georges Guynemer prepares for take-off. *(Below)*
He sits in the cockpit, warming up his Spad. The famous
Stork insignia is on the fuselage.

they were able to rescue him.

In the fall of 1917 Guynemer's escadrille was stationed near Ypres in western Belgium. A series of bloody skirmishes between the English and the Germans in that area had resulted in only slight changes in the battlelines.

Allied and German airmen fought hard at Ypres, too, and no one fought harder than Guynemer. On the morning of September 11, he took off on patrol. In his Spad, which he called *Le Vieux Charles* (Old Charles), he crossed the German lines accompanied by another French plane.

After a few minutes of flying, Guynemer saw an enemy two-seater below him. Signaling to his companion, Sous-Lieutenant Bozon-Verduraz, that he was going to attack, Guynemer nosed his Spad down. But he overshot his target. Cool and collected as ever, he brought the Spad around for another try. The short delay gave the German two-seater a chance to dive away. Guynemer went after it. And that was the last time anyone ever saw the famous French ace.

As Guynemer went after the two-seater, Bozon-Verduraz flew north to draw off some enemy fighters. When he came back, Guynemer had disappeared. Bozon-Verduraz returned to the Storks' airfield alone.

There was no news of Guynemer for several days. Then a German pilot claimed that he had shot down the great ace. But in his claim he had both the day of the week and the time of day wrong. The mystery remained unsolved. No trace was ever found of either Guynemer or his plane. And for many years the legend persisted that Georges Guynemer hadn't been killed. The French said he had flown so high that he just couldn't come down again.

The Storks were saddened by the death of their comrade and vowed to avenge his loss. René Fonck, the Stork who eventually scored seventy-five victories and became the leading Allied ace of World War I, led the effort. One of the German planes he shot down was a two-seater flown by a Lieutenant Wisseman, the very man who had claimed he shot down the great Guynemer.

THE INVINCIBLE ALBERT BALL

England's first great air hero of World War I was Captain Albert Ball. His exploits did much to encourage other young Englishmen to join the Royal Flying Corps. He also developed many of the fighting techniques used by that organization.

Albert Ball grew up in Nottingham, a city in the north central part of England. As a boy, Albert had two hobbies. One was tinkering with engines; the other was shooting at targets. Both hobbies were to help him become an ace.

Ball began his military career as a soldier, not an airman. When England declared war, he enlisted in the Sherwood Foresters, a Nottingham infantry regiment to which many of his friends and neighbors belonged. Then after a few months he was assigned to duty in a cyclist corps. While his unit was waiting to be shipped to France, Ball became interested in flying. One day he visited a flying school at Hendon, near London. What he saw there filled him with enthusiasm for airplanes. He promptly signed up for a series of lessons.

Learning to fly was a difficult undertaking for Ball. He had to pay for his lessons himself, and he had little spare time. Since he was still a member of the cyclist corps, his commander expected him to devote a full day to his duties. This meant that he must get up before dawn, ride to Hendon on his motorcycle, and take his flying lesson. Then he had to hurry back to report to his unit in time for morning parade. Fortunately he was doing this during the summer, when the sun rises very early because of England's northern latitude.

Although Albert missed a great deal of sleep, he learned to fly. In October, 1915, he obtained his pilot's certificate. Three months later he was transferred to the Royal Flying Corps and assigned to No. 13 Squadron, which flew B.E. 2s in France.

The B.E. 2 (Blériot Experimental) was a two seater used for reconnaissance and artillery spotting. A slow, lumbering craft, it was no match for the faster, better-armed planes the Germans were putting into the air. Nevertheless, Ball took his B.E. 2 across the German lines, looking for enemy aircraft as well as for enemy troops and guns. This was a risky business. Ball's commanding officer, who considered him a very good aviator, decided to shift the young flier to

A German Albatros

a unit equipped with fighter planes. In May, 1916, Ball was transferred to No. 11 Squadron. The pilots of this squadron were flying Nieuports, the same fast, maneuverable single-seater that Georges Guynemer used to such good advantage.

Two weeks after Ball joined No. 11 Squadron, the new fighter pilot downed his first German plane. The victim was an Albatros D. I, a German fighter. During that same patrol Ball forced another enemy plane to land.

British rules for scoring aerial victories were as strict as those of the French. Witnesses had to confirm the fact that a plane had been shot down. Because

British pilots carried out many of their missions behind the German lines, enemy airmen and soldiers were often the only witnesses to their aerial battles.

Albert Ball didn't get a victory that could be confirmed until June 25, 1916. On that day he shot down a balloon that had been observing Allied operations. Then on July 2 he was officially credited with shooting down a Roland C. II, the first of several Rolands that fell before his guns. The Roland was a German reconnaissance plane in which the pilot and observer rode above, rather than below, the upper wing. This placed them in a dangerously exposed position when they met enemy aircraft. The unprotected location of the pilot and observer plus the poor maneuverability and slow rate of climb of the Roland made it an unpopular plane with the members of the German air force. The pilots of the Royal Flying Corps, on the other hand, liked to meet up with a Roland.

As the summer of 1916 progressed, Albert Ball perfected his method of attacking enemy planes. After August, when he downed six enemy planes in five days, the number of victories credited to him increased steadily. Like Guynemer he preferred to fly alone, and he liked to fly straight into the enemy. This was a dangerous method of attack because its success depended on the enemy's turning away at the last moment. The pilot who turned first made a perfect target.

Ball often used another dangerous maneuver with

great success: He would let the enemy pilot get on his tail. Just before the German was close enough to open fire, Ball would turn sharply and come up underneath, in an ideal position to shoot. The Britisher was the perfect example of the cool, skillful fighter pilot.

Until 1916 there had been few British air heroes. Although both France and Germany boasted of their famous aces, British officials felt that paying so much attention to the man who fought in the air was unfair to the man who fought equally hard in the cold and mud of the trenches. They were both fighting the same war.

The British objected to singling out a few spectacular fighter pilots for another reason: It was bad for the morale of the men who flew bombers and reconnaissance planes. They too had important jobs to do although they received little recognition.

As a result of this policy, British fighter pilots were allowed to count their victories, but awards and decorations were presented with a minimum of publicity. The names of individual airmen were seldom mentioned in dispatches from the front. But the feats of flying accomplished by Albert Ball made it impossible to keep his name out of the newspapers. The British people wanted an air hero of their own. Albert Ball was the ideal man for the role.

There was much about Albert Ball that made inter-

Albert Ball

esting reading for his countrymen back in England. He was deeply religious. He played the violin and, because he didn't want to disturb others with his music, lived in a hut of his own instead of in the barracks. He had a garden in which he grew a variety of flowers and vegetables from seeds sent to him by his father. He was one of the few pilots to fly without helmet and goggles.

"I like to feel the wind in my hair," he said.

In spite of his growing list of victories in combat, Ball remained a modest young man. He was apt to say, "I was lucky," when discussing the outcome of an aerial battle. Actually an aggressive approach accounted for many of his successes. Even though he might be outnumbered, he had only one thought when he met enemy aircraft: *attack!* Once, flying alone in his Nieuport, he spotted five German planes. There were no other English pilots near enough to help him if he ran into trouble. Nevertheless, he flew in to attack. Perhaps the German pilots were too surprised at his bold action to fight back. At any rate, here, in Ball's own words, is what happened: "One I got and two I forced down. After this I had to run, for all my ammunition was used."

A few days later he was outnumbered again, this time during a mission to protect some bombers carrying out a surprise raid on German targets. The weather had been bad all day, with rain and mist making it difficult to see very far. The failing light of early evening made it even harder to spot anything moving in the sky. But Ball kept looking. His job as a scout, or fighter pilot, was to drive off any German planes that might endanger the bombers. The bombers of World War I were big, slow planes that made easy targets for enemy gunners.

For some time it looked as if the mission would be uneventful. The sky seemed to be empty of German aircraft. But was it? Squinting into the fading light, Ball saw a speck off in the distance. Then another, and another. There were seven in all. As he drew closer, the specks proved to be a squadron of Rolands flying west.

Dusk was a dangerous time for fighter pilots. They found it difficult to judge distance when moving in to attack. But it was also possible to creep up on an enemy without being seen. Knowing that a surprise attack was his only chance of success, Ball flew after the seven Rolands. With great care he worked himself under the last plane in the formation. No one in the Rolands looked back; they weren't expecting an attack.

When Ball had his gun on the target, he fired. The Rolands scattered. Ball followed his victim until the plane crashed; then he sped away.

But his work for that day was not yet over. The sky, which had earlier been so empty, now seemed full of Rolands. Ahead of him were five more. Fortunately Ball saw them before they saw him. Once more he carefully moved in behind the last plane in the formation. Once more luck was with him. None of the Germans looked back. When he was under his intended victim, he fired. A dozen rounds sent the Roland down.

Three of the remaining Rolands immediately moved to encircle the Nieuport, firing at Ball from all directions. He fired back and hit one of the

Rolands. Then he quickly put his Nieuport into a steep dive. It was wise to leave while he could still get away.

Shortly afterward, Ball was transferred to No. 60 Squadron. The Royal Flying Corps had been reorganizing its squadrons so that each one was equipped with a single type of aircraft. No. 60 was an all-Nieuport squadron. Its members were allowed a great deal of freedom in flying patrols. This meant that Ball could fly alone if he wished, which was what he usually wanted to do. He was willing to take risks and he had confidence in his ability to get himself out of a dangerous situation if one should develop. Every week there was a new Ball story to tell in the mess halls of the Royal Flying Corps. Here is one of them.

One day Ball was flying alone as usual. He had flown some distance behind the German lines before he saw any enemy planes. Then he spotted two and immediately sped in to attack. Although he fired away until all his ammunition was gone, neither of the planes appeared to have suffered much damage. But instead of trying to drive off the audacious British pilot while his guns were no longer to be feared, the two German planes turned and fled.

This was not Ball's idea of how a fight should be conducted. On a pad that he carried in his Nieuport, he wrote a note telling the two enemy pilots what he thought of their tactics. He invited them to return to the same spot the next day to finish the fight in a proper fashion. Then Ball dropped the note over the airfield where he had seen the planes land. That done, he headed for home.

The next day, at the appointed time and place, Ball was waiting for the two German pilots. Would they accept his challenge? He didn't have to wait long for an answer. Below him he saw two planes climbing up to finish the battle. The Englishman swooped down to attack. As he did so three more enemy planes dropped out of the clouds above him. He had been trapped! He had wanted to finish yesterday's fight, but not against five blazing guns.

In spite of the increased odds, Ball continued his attack, twisting and turning and shooting whenever he was within range of one of the five. Then he ran out of ammunition. With his own gun silent, he was uncomfortably aware of the whine of German bullets in the air all around him. Sooner or later one of those bullets would hit him.

The beleaguered English pilot was flying over a large field. Suddenly he cut his throttle and started down in a wobbly descent. He wanted the Germans to think he had been hit. When his plane bumped to a halt, Ball slumped forward, playing the part of a wounded, or perhaps even a dead, aviator. But he kept an eye open.

The German planes swooped low over the field to check on the downed aircraft. Then they landed to claim what they expected to be an easy prize.

Ball's engine had been idling as he waited on the ground. As soon as the last German pilot had left his cockpit, the intrepid Englishman opened the throttle wide and roared off. Behind him the astonished Germans watched their "victory" disappear in the direction of the English lines.

Not all of Ball's exploits were as spectacular as this, but his combat score continued to mount until he was Britain's leading ace. After he had destroyed ten enemy aircraft and forced down twenty, Ball received orders sending him back to England. He left France in October, 1916, and became a Royal Flying Corps instructor. His job was to teach other young men how to become good fighter pilots.

Ball would have preferred to remain in France as long as the war lasted. Believing that he could do more for his country in the air than in the classroom, he soon asked to be returned to a fighter squadron. When his first request was not approved he sent in another, and then another. He asked every important official he met to help him get back to the fighting.

Finally, after several months, his request was granted. He was assigned to No. 56 Squadron as a flight commander, to act as a leader for the less experienced pilots flying with him. Ball arrived in France with his new squadron on April 7, 1917.

The British ace returned to a war that was going

badly for his country. Four and a half months of hard fighting on the Somme River in 1916 had advanced the lines less than ten miles. To hold the territory gained at such a high cost, England launched another offensive early in 1917.

In the meantime the Germans had decided to reorganize their armies on the Western Front. To prepare for the reorganization, they moved back to a newly fortified defensive line, called the Siegfried Line by the Germans and the Hindenburg Line by the Allies. As they withdrew the Germans destroyed everything that would be of use to the advancing English.

Because a better-equipped German air force had kept the reconnaissance planes of the Royal Flying Corps from flying over the German lines, the English knew very little about the enemy's retreat. When surprised English "Tommies" advanced into a completely deserted no man's land, they found that nothing remained to protect them from German artillery barrages. Meanwhile, the enemy troops were safe behind the fortified Hindenburg Line.

In April, 1917, the month Albert Ball returned to France, the British were able to take the long-sought Vimy Ridge near Arras. But once again they had to fight a hard battle to gain only a few miles of territory.

While in England, Albert Ball had been looking forward to flying again in the Nieuport, a plane he thought the best in the air. But the plane used by his new squadron was the S.E. 5, a single-seat fighter introduced in the spring of 1917 and sent first to No. 56 Squadron. The S.E. 5 (Scouting Experimental) was a well-designed plane, but at first its engine caused a great deal of trouble.

Ball made no secret of his preference for the Nieuport. Somewhat to his surprise he was given a Nieuport to use in addition to the S.E. 5. He was flying his beloved Nieuport when he shot down his first enemy plane as a member of No. 56 Squadron.

As the days passed Ball grew more accustomed to the S.E. 5 and began to use it more and more. He was the same aggressive fighter in the S.E. 5 that he had been in the Nieuport. The number of victories credited to him began to climb toward forty.

Early in the evening of May 5, 1917, Ball was flying patrol in his S.E. 5 when he saw two German planes about a thousand feet below him. They were both Albatros fighters with two synchronized machine guns each.

The German pilots spotted the S.E. 5 and began to climb toward it. The two German planes, however, were flying at least a quarter of a mile apart. This made it possible for Ball to attack one before the other could reach the scene of the action.

Selecting the nearer Albatros as his target, Ball put his plane into a steep dive. The S.E. 5 was equipped with both a Lewis machine gun mounted on the upper wing and a Vickers gun synchronized

An S.E. 5 (Scouting Experimental)

to fire through the propeller. Using both guns, Ball
fired at the Albatros until it went down. Then he
turned to meet the second Albatros, which was flying
straight at him.

The distance between the two planes diminished
rapidly, but neither pilot turned aside. The German
was firing both his guns. Ball was using his Vickers.
Unless one of them made a sharp turn, there would
be a head-on crash.

Suddenly oil splashed over Ball's face. His oil line
had been hit. For a few minutes he was completely
blinded. He couldn't see the Albatros and he

couldn't guide his own plane. Frantically he wiped away the oil, fully expecting to crash into the Albatros before he could see what was happening. It seemed an eternity before he got enough of the sticky fluid out of his eyes to be able to open them. The Albatros had vanishd. His own plane was in a dive.

As he pulled back hard on the stick to bring his S.E. 5 up again, Ball looked over the side. Below him on the ground he saw the missing Albatros, smashed to bits. Evidently one of Ball's bullets had found its mark and the Albatros had gone down while the British flier was blinded by the oil.

It had been another lucky escape, but how long could such luck hold out? Ball flew again the next day, May 6, and shot down one more Albatros, scoring his forty-fourth victory.

On May 7 Ball, leading his flight of S.E. 5s, took off for an evening patrol. It had been a dark day with constant drizzling rain. The sky was still full of clouds. It was also full of German planes. Soon aerial battles raged over a wide area. Planes roared in and out of the clouds as opposing pilots tried to dodge the bullets of the enemy and, at the same time, get their own guns lined up for an attack. The skies grew darker, and it became difficult to tell friend from foe. The formation of British planes had been scattered by the fighting, but one of the members of No. 56 Squadron saw Albert Ball's red-nosed S.E. 5 fly eastward into a large cloud.

It was never seen again.

A few days later a German newspaper carried the report that the famous German ace, Manfred von Richthofen, had shot down Albert Ball. Then the Germans announced that Lothar von Richthofen, Manfred's younger brother, had been the one to down the famous English flier.

The men of No. 56 Squadron who returned from the May 7 patrol were sure that neither Manfred nor Lothar had shot down their flying ace. Ball had not been wounded when he disappeared, and his plane did not appear to have suffered any damage in the fierce fighting. The men of No. 56 insisted that he had either run out of gas or been hit by anti-aircraft fire from the ground. No German pilot could have shot down the invincible Albert Ball.

Albert Ball's service to his country was far greater than the forty-four planes he brought down. He flew into combat at a time when the Royal Flying Corps was struggling against a German air force equipped with better planes and better guns. It was an uneven conflict, and British losses were heavy.

In those dark days Ball's great success in attacking the enemy did much to encourage other British pilots. His aggressive fighting methods were widely copied.

Before the war ended several Royal Flying Corps pilots had surpassed Ball's record for the number of enemy planes destroyed. Among them was a daring

Canadian ace, Billy Bishop, who ran up a score of seventy-two victories, an R.F.C. record surpassed only by Edward Mannock.

But by this time the Corps was equipped with better planes and guns. And its fliers were better too, thanks to the example set by Albert Ball.

Canada's greatest ace, Colonel William Bishop, demonstrates the Foster mount that made the Lewis machine gun such an effective weapon on the Nieuport, and later on the S.E. 5. Although Bishop's actual combat service lasted only about six months, he won every British military medal, including the Distinguished Service Order, the Military Cross, and the Victoria Cross. During his last twelve days of combat flying, he scored 25 victories, downing 5 enemy planes on his last afternoon. Canadian aces like Bishop, Raymond Collishaw, and William Barker made a spectacular contribution to the Allied war in the air.

MANFRED VON RICHTHOFEN AND HIS FLYING CIRCUS

Germany produced the aviator who became the leading ace of World War I. Manfred Freiherr von Richthofen shot down eighty enemy planes in aerial combat. Besides being a skillful fighter pilot, the German ace won fame as a commander. The Richthofen "Circus," which he organized and led, was the best aerial fighting unit of the war.

Manfred von Richthofen grew up in Silesia, at that time a province of Prussia. Silesia was a region of few cities, and its vast forests were full of wild game. Hunting became the favorite sport of Manfred and his younger brother, Lothar, who was also to become a famous ace. Both of the brothers were expert marksmen. There is little doubt that the hours they spent stalking game in the Silesian forests helped them to become skillful fighter pilots.

When Manfred was eleven years old he was sent

to a military cadet school. His father had been an officer in the German army and he wanted his older son to follow in his footsteps. Manfred, a strong, active boy, won several prizes in sports but none in his studies.

After cadet school, Manfred attended the Royal Military Academy and then the War Academy in Berlin. In 1911 he joined the 1st Regiment of Uhlans. The Uhlans were mounted soldiers or cavalrymen who acted as scouts, riding ahead to locate the enemy.

When World War I began, Manfred von Richthofen's regiment was stationed near his home in Silesia. His first war-time assignment transferred him to the Polish village of Kielce to watch for a Russian advance in that area. Each day for a week he sent one of his troopers riding back to the German base with a dispatch. Then, because Germany had decided to defeat France first, von Richthofen's regiment, with its horses, moved by train to the Western Front. When they reached the German border, the Uhlans mounted their horses and traveled with the German army across Luxembourg and Belgium into France.

As the French army fell back before the German advance, the Uhlans were sent ahead to locate the new French positions. This they did by riding into the woods until they drew the enemy's fire. Then they tried to determine the strength and exact location of the French troops.

When the French retreat ended, both sides dug

Manfred von Richthofen

the trenches from which they were to fight for many months. Because there was no longer a need for mounted scouts, Manfred von Richthofen became a supply officer.

The former cavalryman disliked his new job. He is said to have written to his commander: "I have not come to war to collect cheese and eggs, but for another reason."

He realized that the day of the cavalryman was over. Observers in airplanes rather than Uhlans on horseback were now the eyes of the army. Manfred asked to be trained as an observer. At that time in the German Aviation Service pilots were low-ranking men who flew planes. The observer was the important man in a military aircraft. He outranked the pilot and was in charge of the mission.

The training course for observers took a month to complete. It included fifteen hours of flying training so that the observers could supervise the work of the pilots. Manfred von Richthofen had never flown before. But as soon as he became used to the noise of the engine and the cold wind blowing through the open cockpit, he decided he liked flying.

His first assignment as an observer was on the Eastern Front, where the Germans and Austrians were driving the Russians back from Hungary and Poland. On the Eastern Front the opposing armies were not as evenly matched as in the West. The Germans could usually muster a stronger and better organized force than the Russians, but the Russian army, in turn, was stronger than the Austrian army. As a result, the battlelines moved back and forth and there was little of the static trench warfare that developed on the Western Front.

Von Richthofen made daily reconnaissance flights behind the Russian lines, riding in the rear cockpit of a two-seater Albatros. His unit kept the 6th

Austrian Corps informed of the enemy's movements.

When the Russian withdrawal was completed in August, 1915, von Richthofen received orders sending him back to the Western Front. Germany, fighting a war on two fronts, had to shift her soldiers and airmen from one front to another as they were needed. The young airman was assigned to a bomber unit. In a bomber, an observer helped the pilot locate targets; he also dropped the bombs. But von Richthofen disliked flying in the big, slow bombing plane. He called it an "apple barge." Whenever he could he flew as an observer in an Albatros.

The day that Manfred von Richthofen shot down his first plane he was in an Albatros on an observation mission behind the French lines. His pilot overtook the enemy ship, a Farman, and skillfully flew alongside it while von Richthofen fired away with his machine gun. He hit the Farman and it went plummeting to the ground. The future ace was surprised to see it go. Later, in describing the fight, he said: "I couldn't believe my eyes."

Germany, like France, publicized the exploits of her airmen. Newspapers and magazines carried colorful accounts of aerial battles and often mentioned the names of pilots who had fought in them. Victory scores appeared regularly. The German equivalent of the ace was the *Kanone,* but a German pilot had to shoot down ten enemy aircraft to attain that exalted title.

Oswald Boelcke

German rules for crediting victories were as rigid as those of France and England. There had to be positive evidence of destruction. As a result, von Richthofen was not allowed to count the Farman as a victory. He had brought it down behind the French lines, where he could obtain no proof of its destruction.

In the fall of 1915 Manfred met Oswald Boelcke, the most famous flier in the German Aviation Service. Boelcke had already shot down four planes. Having learned how difficult it was to down an enemy airplane, Manfred asked, "How do you do it?" Boelcke, who was soon to become Germany's first ace, explained how it was done: "I fly close to my man, aim well, fire, and then he falls down."

Von Richthofen remarked that enemy planes were very difficult to hit, even if one aimed well. Boelcke pointed out that he flew in a Fokker Eindecker, a fighter plane equipped with a machine gun that fired through the propeller.

That was the answer. Manfred von Richthofen decided he would learn to fly a fighter. He had had enough of slow, two-seater aircraft.

The pilot's course was a long one. In order to save time, Manfred asked a friend to teach him to fly. When he had learned enough to make a successful solo flight, he went to a training unit for further instruction. The pilots of the German Aviation Service had to pass a series of examinations more difficult than the examinations given to French and British fliers. On Christmas Day, 1915, Manfred passed his final test. In March he returned to the Western Front, but this time as a pilot. He was not yet a fighter pilot, however. Again he was assigned to an Albatros. But now, instead of riding in the rear cockpit as an observer, he sat up front and did the flying.

The only gun carried by the Albatros was in the rear cockpit with the observer. Von Richthofen wanted to be able to use a gun too, so he had a second machine gun mounted on the upper wing of the Albatros. His plane was one of the first to carry more than one gun.

It wasn't long before an enemy plane fell victim to von Richthofen's gun. This time it was a French Nieuport, but once again the German pilot received no credit. Like the first plane he had shot down, the Nieuport fell behind the French lines.

In the summer of 1916 Manfred moved back to the Eastern Front. There he met Oswald Boelcke again. The famous German flier was visiting airfields, looking for outstanding pilots for a special fighter unit he was forming. "Would you like to go with me?" he asked the young von Richthofen.

The answer, of course, was yes. The decision marked the turning point in Manfred's career.

The new unit was the famous *Jagdstaffel 2,* or *Jasta 2* as it was usually called. An all-fighter squadron, its mission was to protect reconnaissance and bomber aircraft. Oswald Boelcke became *Jasta 2's* teacher as well as its commander. His rules for air fighting were so effective that they were still being used at the outset of World War II.

"Keep your eyes on the enemy. Watch out for tricks. If you are taken by surprise, turn to meet your adversary. The best place for an attack is from behind." With shrewd advice of this sort Boelcke turned his men into skillful fighter pilots.

On his first combat mission as a member of *Jasta 2,* Richthofen shot down an English plane. It fell behind the German lines. Determined to examine his victim on the ground, the excited pilot almost wrecked his own ship while landing. But there was no question this time. The future ace was officially credited with victory number one on September 17, 1916.

It was Boelcke's custom to present a silver victory cup to each man after he shot down his first plane. When von Richthofen received his that night, he decided to start a cup collection of his own. In it there would be a cup for each plane he shot down. He sent his order for the first one to a jeweler in Berlin. The inscription was to read:

1. Vickers 2. 17.9.16.

By November 9, 1916, he had eight cups.

In the meantime, the famous leader of *Jasta 2* had been killed in a midair collision with one of his own men. Boelcke's death was a severe blow to the German Aviation Service. He had done much to build up its strength. Even his enemies mourned the German ace's untimely death. They considered him a courageous and honorable fighter. Planes of the Royal Flying Corps flew above the town of Cambrai, where Boelcke's funeral was held. The British pilots dropped several wreaths. One of the inscriptions read: "To the memory of Captain Boelcke, our brave and chivalrous foe. From the British Royal Flying Corps."

The squadron that Boelcke had taught so well, renamed *Jagdstaffel Boelcke,* continued to knock Allied planes from the air. Manfred von Richthofen was now downing enemy planes at the rate of one

A German Albatros photographed from above during a dogfight. The German insignia, a black cross, is painted on both wings.

a week. He flew an Albatros D. II, an exceptionally speedy, two-gun fighter. Of the planes that the French and the British were using in the fall of 1916, only the Nieuports and the Sopwith Pups, which were few in number, could stand up to the Albatros D. II.

In his encounters with the enemy, Richthofen took advantage of the speed and maneuverability of his Albatros. He liked to attack from behind and below. While he was in that location, enemy gunners had difficulty aiming at him, but *he* was in a good position to shoot at them. Most of the planes he shot down were slow two-seaters that didn't put up much fight. One day, however, he had an opponent who put his skill to a real test.

Von Richthofen was flying just behind the German lines when a British fighter plane zeroed in on him from above. The pilot of the fighter was Major Lanoe Hawker, one of the aces of the Royal Flying Corps and a flier of great skill and daring.

A split second before Hawker drew close enough to fire, Manfred realized that an enemy ship had come down on his tail. He banked sharply. His only hope was to get around behind Hawker. The British pilot was just as determined to come up behind the Albatros. The result was a series of circles as both pilots tried to get into position to fire. They circled to the right; they circled to the left. At times they were so close to one another that von Richthofen could see into the cockpit of the English plane. Their maneuvers brought them down from 8,000 to 3,000 feet.

Here at last was an adversary worthy of the German ace. But unfortunately for Hawker they were behind the German lines. The British flier had to break away while he still had enough fuel to get back to his own lines. When he went into a diving turn, Richthofen followed closely. Hawker tried to dodge the fire coming from the Albatros, but he was too low to have much room for maneuvering. A bullet struck him in the head, killing him. It was Richthofen's eleventh victory in combat.

In a letter to his mother a few days later, the German ace wrote of Hawker: "He gave me the hardest fight I have experienced so far."

Aerial duels such as the one with Hawker enhanced von Richthofen's reputation as a skillful fighter pilot. Soon he was given his own squadron to command, *Jasta 11*. Although the men of *Jasta 11* seemed to be good fliers, not one of them had downed an enemy plane. Their new commander soon changed that. He taught them all the valuable lessons he had learned from his own teacher, Oswald Boelcke. The day came when six planes from *Jasta 11* were able to shoot down thirteen enemy planes with only slight damage to themselves.

The men of *Jasta 11* flew the new Albatros D. III. Their planes were painted a bright red, and all of them except Manfred's also bore markings in another color. His plane was all red. British reconnaissance

Baron von Richthofen and his celebrated Jasta 11 line up for inspection.

pilots had reason to fear the sight of a red Albatros. In March, 1917, when the British were desperate for information concerning the location of the German army, then in a slow retreat toward the Hindenburg Line, *Jasta 11* wiped out a whole flight of observation planes. And when the British began their drive toward Vimy Ridge in April, *Jasta 11* was waiting to pounce on the Royal Flying Corps planes sent to check on German defenses. Although the squadron had been in existence only since January, *Jasta 11* scored its one-hundredth victory on April 23. Manfred von Richthofen himself shot down his forty-seventh plane on the 23rd. He was now Germany's leading ace.

In March, 1917, Manfred's younger brother, Lothar, had joined *Jasta 11*. Like Manfred, Lothar had been a cavalryman and an observer before becoming a pilot. And like Manfred he became an outstanding fighter pilot. During his first month with *Jasta 11*, Lothar shot down twenty enemy planes.

The famous Richthofen "Circus" was formed in June, 1917, when *Jasta 11* and three other squadrons became *Jagdgeschwader 1* under the leadership of Manfred von Richthofen. *Jagdgeschwader 1* was to be moved along the front wherever it was needed to maintain German air supremacy. Pilots of the Royal Flying Corps had been calling the planes of *Jasta 11* "Richthofen's Circus" because of their bright red color. Now the term was widely applied to the formidable air-fighting formations of *Jagdgeschwader 1*.

Early in July, not long after the Circus went into action, an observer in a British two-seater fired at a red Albatros during a furious aerial battle near the British lines. The Albatros was about 300 yards away, too far for accurate shooting. But much to the British observer's surprise the German craft went into a dive. Von Richthofen himself was the pilot of the red Albatros, and he had been hit in the head.

The wound was a serious one. Von Richthofen, blinded and at times unconscious, lost control of his Albatros. As the plane neared the ground he managed to pull back on the stick and bring it out of a steep dive. Luckily, he had come down behind the German

A squadron of fast Albatros scouts belonging to Richtho-fen's "Flying Circus."

lines. He made a bumpy landing and staggered from the cockpit. Then he collapsed.

The German soldiers who ran to his aid thought the famous ace was dead. He was covered with blood. But von Richthofen surprised them. Not only was he alive, he insisted on being taken back to his own headquarters.

It was the first time Manfred von Richthofen had been injured in almost three years of fighting. This is what he wrote about his wound: "I had quite a good-sized hole. In one spot, as big as a dollar, the bare white skull bone lay exposed. My thick Richthofen skull had proved itself bulletproof."

At the end of July he resumed command of the Circus. Three weeks later he was well enough to fly. On his very first venture into the air he shot down a Nieuport, his fifty-eighth victory.

Late in August, 1917, the pilots of *Jagdgeschwader 1* received new airplanes. They were triplanes designed by Anthony Fokker. The three wings of his triplane gave the craft more lifting power than the one wing of a monoplane or the two wings of a biplane. The new plane was a maneuverable, fast-climbing machine. When Manfred von Richthofen flew in it for the first time on September 1, he scored his sixtieth victory.

The dreaded Circus continued to patrol the skies above the Western Front, and its pilots continued to shoot down enemy planes, though not in such large numbers as before. The Royal Flying Corps was acquiring new and faster aircraft. At the same time the Germans were having less success in keeping up with the aircraft production race. Even the Fokker triplane was slower than some of the new British models.

On the Eastern Front, Russia had suffered a long

series of demoralizing defeats. A revolution broke out in that country in March, 1917. A new government replaced the absolute monarchy of the Czar, but Russian losses on the battlefields remained high. After another revolution in which the Bolsheviks under Lenin took over the government, Russia signed an armistice with Germany and withdrew from the war in December, 1917.

Germany, free at last to concentrate all her forces on one front, launched a massive attack against British positions on the Somme River in March, 1918. As the German army charged forward on the ground, the Circus battled the Royal Flying Corps in the air. Von Richthofen flew often, sometimes shooting down two or even three planes a day. He seemed to have regained all the skill he had before he was wounded. On April 20 he shot down his eightieth plane.

The next morning there was a delay in take-off because of a heavy ground mist. When it lifted, five planes followed von Richthofen's red Fokker triplane into the air. They were going out to look for enemy reconnaissance craft, for they knew the British were trying to locate some new German army positions.

The same ground mist that delayed the German patrol also delayed a British patrol headed for the same area. One of the flight leaders of the British patrol was Captain Arthur Royal Brown, a Canadian who had studied aviation at the Wright Flying School in Dayton, Ohio. In 1915 he joined the Royal Naval

Captain Arthur Brown, the Canadian pilot credited with the death of Baron von Richthofen.

Air Service. A flying accident kept him out of combat until 1917. But after his arrival in France he rapidly developed into a fearless pilot and an exceptionally good flight leader.

The flight paths of the British and German patrols actually crossed. But they were flying at different altitudes and they were screened from one another by clouds. When the German formation neared the British lines it was spotted by sharp-eyed anti-aircraft gunners. The white puffs of the bursting British anti-aircraft shells told Brown that there were enemy planes near by. He led his flight down to attack. Von Richthofen, at the head of the German formation, turned to meet the oncoming British fighters. The battle was on.

Twisting, turning, climbing, diving, the opposing

German and British pilots maneuvered for position. While getting ready to fire their guns, they had to be sure that they themselves weren't fired upon. The pilot who forgot to look behind him was in trouble. In fact, in this fight he was in trouble if he couldn't look in all directions at once. Planes were coming in on every side.

After some opening skirmishes, Manfred von Richthofen set off after a British Camel that had become separated from the main action. The Camel belonged to Captain Brown's flight. Like a mother hen the Canadian flight leader flew to the rescue. The German ace was closing in on his target. All his attention was concentrated on getting into a good firing position. He did not see the plane diving at him from almost directly above his head.

Brown was not in an ideal position for an attack. As he roared past the red triplane he fired a short burst. Evidently it was enough. The pilot in the triplane turned around in a startled manner. Then he slumped forward. The triplane went down on the British side of the lines.

To this day there are members of an Australian anti-aircraft battery who insist that the great ace fell to their guns, fired from the ground. Officially, Captain Brown is credited with destroying the red triplane and ending the career of Manfred von Richthofen.

The German ace was buried with full military

An Australian squadron buries the greatest of German aces with full military honors.

honors by No. 3 Squadron, Australian Flying Corps, near whose airfield he fell. Like Oswald Boelcke before him, Manfred von Richthofen was respected by the Allied fliers as a skillful pilot and a courageous fighter.

The flying Circus fought on after the death of its great leader, but the tide of battle was turning. American men and supplies were arriving to help the Allies. More and better Allied planes flew over the Western Front, where there were fewer German planes and pilots to drive them off. And Germany had lost its best aerial fighter and commander, Manfred von Richthofen.

RAOUL LUFBERY AND THE ESCADRILLE LAFAYETTE

In his farewell address the first President of the United States, George Washington, told his countrymen to avoid entanglements with other nations, and for many years his advice was followed. Even in 1914, when World War I began, President Woodrow Wilson hastened to issue a proclamation pledging his country to strict neutrality. The United States would favor neither side.

America had no intention of becoming involved in a European war. In fact, she was totally unprepared to do so. In 1914 the Army numbered only 87,000 men, and they had little equipment except their rifles. The Navy boasted a fleet of battleships, but it had few smaller vessels. And the United States lacked a single airplane suitable for combat.

Even though tradition and practical considerations prompted the government to adopt a neutral role, individual Americans were involved in the conflict almost from the beginning, and most of them were on the side of the Allies. Some of the Americans were already in Europe when the fighting began. William Thaw, for example, had gone to France to sell an automatic stabilizer invented by his brother. Bert Hall was a taxi driver in Paris. James Bach, a mechanical engineer, had lived and worked in Europe for several years.

Other young Americans quickly sailed for France to offer their services. In this group were two brothers, Kiffin and Paul Rockwell; Robert Soubiran, who had been a racing-car driver; and Didier Masson, a former stunt flier. Two others, William Prince and Frazier Curtis, enrolled in a flying school before leaving the United States because they wanted to serve as aviators.

On August 21, 1914, several of the American volunteers were inducted into the French Foreign Legion. If the young men had joined the regular French army, they would have been required to give up their American citizenship. That, of course, they did not wish to do. The French Foreign Legion, which was made up of nationals of many countries, asked only that a man obey his commanding officer.

Wearing the red cap and blue overcoat of the Foreign Legion, the Americans marched to the front in October, 1914. Although not many of them could fly, they had already begun to discuss the possibility of forming an all-American squadron of aviators. During their stay at the front they saw some of the first air battles of the war and their desire to fly for France became stronger.

When William Thaw, James Bach, and Bert Hall were sent to a rest area behind the lines, they visited a French airfield and asked to be transferred to aviation. A few weeks later, Bach and Hall, neither of whom could fly an airplane, received transfers. Thaw, who was already a pilot, did not. But another visit to the airfield resulted in a transfer for Thaw, too.

Meanwhile, Norman Prince had arrived in France after completing his flight training. He immediately began to promote the idea of an American aviation squadron. Many of the Americans serving in the Foreign Legion and in the American Ambulance Corps (a volunteer organization) said they would like to join such a squadron.

At first the Americans received little encouragement from the French government. What if one of the foreign aviators should turn out to be a spy? And besides, French soldiers ought to be given a chance to transfer to aviation before outsiders were accepted. Undaunted by this attitude, Prince continued to contact important French officials and influential Americans living in France. As a result of his efforts, the Franco-American Committee was organized to work for the formation of an American air squadron. In July, 1915, the members of the committee met with the general in charge of French military aviation.

After listening to the committee, the general agreed that the squadron should be formed.

But nothing happened. In January, 1916, there still was no American squadron. But Thaw, Bach, and Hall and several other Americans had transferred to the *Aviation Militaire,* completed flight training, and joined French aviation squadrons. One day William Thaw told his commander about the plans for an American squadron. The commander, Captain Georges Thenault, became so interested in the idea that he submitted a request to take charge of the new squadron when it was formed.

The Franco-American Committee went to work again. Finally, in April, orders were issued establishing the *Escadrille Américaine N. 124* under the command of Captain Thenault. The first Americans reported for duty at Luxeuil, France, on April 18. They were Victor Chapman, James McConnell, Norman Prince, and Kiffin Rockwell. William Thaw, Elliott Cowden, and Bert Hall arrived a few days later.

Luxeuil had been chosen for the Americans' first airfield because it was located on a quiet sector of the front. The fliers of the new escadrille were to protect the bombers based at Luxeuil while they developed the teamwork essential for a good fighting unit.

The *Escadrille Américaine* flew its first patrol on the morning of May 13, 1916, with Kiffin Rockwell leading a formation of five Nieuports. No enemy planes were sighted, but on May 18 Rockwell scored the escadrille's first victory when he sent a German observation ship crashing to the earth.

The next day the Americans were ordered to Verdun, where the German army was pushing hard at the French fortifications. The French maintained a continuous patrol over the battle area to drive off German observation planes before they could locate French troops and guns. The patrols also protected the French planes that were dropping bombs on the enemy. The *Escadrille Américaine,* like the other escadrilles at Verdun, was assigned a certain time, place, and altitude for its patrols.

The Americans began operations from their new airfield at Behonne on May 22. Bert Hall, flying patrol on May 23, became the second member of the *Escadrille Américaine* to down an enemy observation plane. The next day William Thaw scored victory number three, a fighter. But the modest Thaw explained later that it was no great accomplishment since the unfortunate victim never saw him.

Even though the *Escadrille Américaine* was now flying at the front, there were some American pilots still serving in French squadrons or in training. Several of these men transferred to the *Escadrille Américaine* during May and June, 1917. Raoul Lufbery, who became the escadrille's leading ace, reported for duty on May 24.

Raoul Lufbery's life had already been full of adven-

Raoul Lufbery

ture. He was born in France in 1885. His father was an American. His mother, who died when Raoul was very young, was French. At nineteen young Lufbery left France to see the world. He traveled through the Balkans and Germany, paying his way by working at odd jobs. He was a waiter in a restaurant; he helped unload boats; for a time he was a racing-car driver. He also worked on a ship sailing between Germany and ports in Africa. When he could find no other job, he became a dishwasher. Later, in describing his experiences, he said: "I was never out of funds for more than twenty-four hours."

Lufbery's travels eventually took him to the United States, where he planned to visit his father, who had settled in Wallingford, Connecticut. But his father, too, was something of a traveler. He was a dealer in stamps and traveled in search of rare ones for his collection. Knowing nothing of his son's plans, he had sailed for Europe shortly before Raoul arrived in Wallingford.

Raoul remained in Wallingford for a while, but his father did not return. So the young man continued his travels. He went to Cuba and from there to New Orleans, where he worked in a bakery. At his next stop, San Francisco, he was a waiter in a hotel. He then enlisted in the United States Army and was sent to the Philippines. By the time his two-year enlistment was up, he had become the best rifle marksman in his regiment.

After his discharge from the Army, Lufbery went to Japan and from there to China. He wandered through China for months, always curious, always eager for new adventures. For a time he had a position in the Chinese customs service. Then wanderlust carried him to India. In Bombay he was employed as a ticket agent.

At Saigon, in Indochina, Raoul saw his first airplane. He had heard about the Wright Brothers and their flight at Kitty Hawk, and he knew a little about gliders. But he had never actually seen an airplane.

Eager, as always, to learn about new things, he followed a crowd of curious natives to a field on the outskirts of a city. There a French stunt flier was to put on an exhibition flight. The flier was Marc Pourpe. His plane was an old Blériot.

When Lufbery arrived at the field, Pourpe was trying to set up a tent hangar to shelter his plane. But he was having trouble explaining to a group of local laborers just how it should be done. Because a storm was brewing, he wanted to get the tent up as quickly as possible. Observing the situation, Lufbery went up to the harassed flier and said: "I can tell them what to do. Let me help you."

He quickly organized the workmen, and the tent was erected. That was the beginning of Lufbery's friendship with Marc Pourpe and of his career in aviation. As it happened, Pourpe's mechanic had recently become ill and returned to France. Pourpe needed someone to take care of his plane. Would Lufbery like the job? He would! He became a mechanic under Pourpe's instruction and soon mastered his new calling. Raoul enjoyed working with engines. He kept the old Blériot running smoothly as they traveled through China and the Orient, putting on aerial exhibitions which thrilled the crowds of people who came to see the amazing flying machine.

While they were in Egypt, Pourpe flew the Blériot up the Nile as far as Khartoum and back, a remarkable flight for those days. Lufbery preceded or followed him the whole way, traveling by boat, raft, train, camel, donkey, and sometimes on foot.

In the summer of 1914 Lufbery and Marc Pourpe returned to France to buy a new and larger airplane. Their plan was to continue the exhibition flights as they traveled from one country to another. But they never bought the new plane and they never resumed their travels. For on August 3 Germany declared war on France.

The two friends went at once to enlist in the *Aviation Militaire*. Only Pourpe was accepted. Because Lufbery was an American citizen, the only branch of service open to him was the French Foreign Legion. He promptly enlisted in it as an infantryman.

Once in uniform, Lufbery requested a transfer to the *Aviation Militaire*. He wanted to serve with his friend. With Pourpe's help, Lufbery was transferred to Escadrille M.S. 23, and he became Marc Pourpe's mechanic. The two had served together for a short time when, on December 2, 1914, Marc Pourpe was killed in combat.

The grief-stricken Lufbery vowed he would avenge his friend. He would become a pilot.

Lufbery's request for flying training was approved. Because of his determination and his work with Pourpe, it took him only a few weeks to earn his certificate at the flying school at Chartres. The new pilot's first assignment was to a squadron which flew

Voisin bombers. The Voisin was a slow plane built to carry a large load of bombs. For six months Lufbery flew it on bombing missions.

Flying a Voisin, however, was not what he had in mind when he vowed he would become a pilot and avenge the death of Marc Pourpe. He wanted to fly a speedy fighter and drive the enemy from the skies. He sent in another request, this time for training as a fighter pilot. It, too, was approved.

Although Raoul Lufbery was to become one of the most skillful and successful fighter pilots, he found it difficult to transfer from the Voisin to the Nieuport. He seemed to lack the delicate touch needed to maneuver the tricky Nieuport. In fact, he did so badly that his instructors recommended that he remain a bomber pilot. "Your hand is too heavy to make a good pursuit pilot," they told him.

Lufbery refused to give up. He was determined to fly the Nieuport. He practiced the required maneuvers over and over until he had completely mastered the plane. Then he was sent to the *Escadrille Améri-caine* at Verdun. When Lufbery arrived at Verdun, the still inexperienced Americans were taking an active part in the fighting. They often returned from their patrols with big holes in the fabric of their planes, with wires and braces cut, and with controls damaged. The German fliers were very skillful and daring. But the Americans improved rapidly. They developed and practiced combat tactics and learned

Left to right: Walter Lovell, Edmond C. Genet, Raoul Lufbery, and James McConnell discuss combat tactics.

to take advantage of the maneuverability of their speedy Nieuports.

Raoul Lufbery downed his first enemy ship on July 30, 1916. Returning from a patrol, he sighted the German craft heading for the French lines. Lufbery was flying alone. He immediately swung toward the enemy ship and the battle began. After a short fight, during which Lufbery did most of the shooting, the German went spinning to the earth in flames. Lufbery had begun to avenge the death of Marc Pourpe.

On August 4, Lufbery shot down two more enemy planes. Four days later another fell before his diving attack. The man who had been the despair of his instructors was becoming one of the best fighter pilots in the *Escadrille Américaine.*

His fifth victim was a three-place Aviatik. This plane, the work horse of the German Aviation Service, was produced in both two- and three-place models for light bombing and low-altitude work. Although the Aviatik's tail gunner was aiming a steady stream of bullets at him, Lufbery managed to fly under the tail of the plane, shooting up at it as he went. The unexpected attack was too much for the Aviatik. It side-slipped and went into a spin. As the big ship fell in flames, its wings snapped off one after the other. The sky seemed full of falling pieces of airplane.

With five enemy aircraft destroyed, Raoul Lufbery was now an ace—America's first. He became a hero. The newspapers in both France and America were full of his pictures and stories of his aerial exploits. Children were named after him. He received bundles of letters from admirers. Raoul had always been a modest, unassuming person. Being a hero didn't change him.

He loved to fly and his plane seemed to be a part of him. One of his fellow pilots said of Lufbery: "He was one of the rare men whose machine was a continuation of his arms and legs. He flew like a bird, by impulse, with no thought of how it was done."

The members of the escadrille who were not on patrol would often wait at the hangars to watch Lufbery return from a mission. He always kept his altitude on the way back in the hope of spotting one last enemy plane. When he reached the field, he would throttle back and descend in beautiful spirals until he was low enough for a landing. Sometimes he would entertain his audience with an intricate series of stunts. He was considered the best in the escadrille at stunting.

Lufbery felt that some of his success in combat was due to luck. He often said that three-fourths of the time he was just plain lucky. But he worked hard. He flew alone a great deal and waited patiently for an opportunity to pounce on an enemy plane. He tried always to be in a favorable position for attack when he went into action. In attacking a two-seater, he aimed at the blind spots on either side of the front gun. As an alternative he would pull up underneath and rake both cockpits before the rear gunner could go into action. He was careful to stay out of the range of the rear gunners. They had shot down too many Allied planes.

A favorite maneuver of his was to circle slowly, high up in the sun, until he spotted an enemy formation serenely slipping along below him. Because of the brilliance of the sun, pilots were often unable to see their adversaries. Thus Lufberry could take the enemy completely by surprise. Coming down in a thunderous dive, he sometimes attacked formations of as many as six ships. His daring and courage and the skill with which he directed his plane in its dive often were enough to scatter the enemy fliers.

When he himself was under attack by an enemy ship, Lufbery would try to hold his dangerous position until the enemy pilot closed in for the kill. Then at the last minute he would whip around to the enemy's tail and proceed to inflict the damage that had been intended for him a few seconds earlier. When he couldn't get away from a pursuing plane, he would force his Nieuport into a swaying movement, which made it a difficult target for enemy gunners to hit.

Six, seven, eight—the number of Lufbery's victories increased. And for every downed plane that could be credited to him officially, there was another that could not be counted because it had been shot down behind enemy lines with no witness to the battle. The fliers of the *Escadrille Américaine* were held to the same strict scoring rules observed by the other squadrons of the *Aviation Militaire*.

In the fall of 1916 the battle of Verdun was drawing to a close. The French had refused to retreat. The *Escadrille Américaine* moved back to Luxeuil, where once again it protected the French bombers that used Luxeuil as a base. The American fliers were given a newer model of the Nieuport to fly—the Nieuport

Men of the Escadrille Lafayette. Seated (center): Didier Masson with Soda on his lap, William Thaw playing with Whiskey, Captain Georges Thenault, and Raoul Lufbery.

17, which carried a Vickers machine gun synchronized to fire through the propeller and a Lewis gun mounted on the top wing. The first 17s to arrive at Luxeuil, however, had only the Lewis gun in place.

At Luxeuil the escadrille acquired its famous mascot—the lion cub, Whiskey. Whiskey, after chewing his way through innumerable blankets and curtains, and even a uniform or two, grew into a gentle lion that followed the pilots around like a big dog.

Lufbery, who was especially fond of Whiskey, claimed that the lion really thought he was a dog. Later, the Americans obtained another lion cub, Soda, as a companion for Whiskey, but Whiskey remained the squadron favorite.

The *Escadrille Américaine* moved a second time that fall—to Cachy, north of Paris on the Somme River. Here the Americans got their first real taste of combat living conditions. When it rained, the mud was knee-deep. The roof of the barracks leaked. At first there were no blankets. The pilots had to sleep in their flying clothes to keep warm. There were no stoves or pots and pans for cooking. The Americans ate with the squadrons that had been at Cachy long enough to secure cooking equipment.

It was at Cachy that the escadrille adopted the famous insignia, the head of an Indian chief, that was to decorate all its airplanes. The idea came from the Seminole Indian trademark on an ammunition box. One of the French mechanics attached to the escadrille painted the insignia on the Nieuports. When the fliers decided that the colors of the Seminole chief's headdress didn't show up well enough from a distance, the headdress of a Sioux chief was used instead. From a distance it could be seen as distinct spots of red, white, and blue, which pleased the Americans.

Naturally, the activities of the *Escadrille Améri- caine* received a great deal of attention in newspapers

Lufbery in his Nieuport 17 receives a send-off from Didier Masson, Whiskey, and Robert Soubiran (far left). The colorful Indian-head insignia is prominent on the fuselage.

and magazines back in the United States. The stories made the German ambassador in Washington angry. The United States was supposed to be a neutral country. How could a neutral country have a squadron of airmen shooting down German planes in France?

To avoid putting the United States in an embarrassing position, government officials suggested that the squadron name be changed from *Escadrille Américaine* to *Escadrille des Volontaires*, or squadron of volunteers. The Americans in France didn't like the new name. They thought it dull and colorless. One of them, Edmond Genêt, suggested that the squadron be called the *Escadrille Lafayette* in honor of the Marquis de Lafayette, who so generously and gallantly served America in the Revolutionary War. Everyone liked the idea. On December 6, 1916, *Escadrille Lafayette* became the official name of the American squadron.

Changing the name of the *Escadrille Américaine* solved only one of the many problems faced by the United States as she tried to remain a neutral country. Germany's invasion and occupation of neutral Belgium had caused many Americans to favor the Allies. This feeling became more widespread after a German submarine sank the liner *Lusitania* in 1915, with a loss of 128 American lives. Germany was also suspected of sabotaging munitions factories, but a message she sent to the Mexican government early in 1917 did the most harm to relations between Germany and the United States. In the message, which was intercepted and published, Germany asked Mexico to enter the war and promised her territory belonging to the United States. A few weeks later, on April 6, 1917, President Woodrow Wilson signed a formal declaration of war against Germany.

When the members of the *Escadrille Lafayette* heard the news they said: "We will all be transferred to the American Air Service within a month."

The American pilots were eager to wear the uniform of their own country, and the French government agreed to release them. But it was some months before the United States Air Service was ready for their transfer.

In April, 1917, the Air Service was woefully unprepared to fight a war. It had less than 250 aircraft, none of which could compete with the planes fighting in Europe. It had only one squadron ready for any sort of action.

While the Air Service organized for combat, the members of the *Escadrille Lafayette* continued to fly for France as they had always done. Moving from one

Aerial view of the airfield at Ham where the Escadrille Lafayette was based in the early spring of 1917.

airfield to another as their services were needed by the French or English armies, they accounted for a growing number of destroyed enemy planes.

In just one day—October 24, 1917—Raoul Lufbery fought three big air battles in which he shot down six enemy planes. Other pilots flying near by saw them go down, but only one was seen by a qualified observer. So Raoul's score for the day was one.

In December the United States Air Service announced it was ready to accept the pilots of the *Escadrille Lafayette*. The French government released them promptly, but the still-floundering American Air Service did not officially take over until February. On February 18, 1918, the *Escadrille Lafayette* was disbanded. While flying for France, its gallant pilots had scored fifty-seven confirmed victories over the enemy. Nine of its members had been killed in action. The first four men to report for duty with the escadrille—Victor Chapman, James McConnell, Norman Prince, and Kiffin Rockwell—were among the nine.

Raoul Lufbery was credited with seventeen planes shot down, the most of anyone in the escadrille. He got them all behind the enemy lines. His fellow pilots insisted that he had shot down at least twice that many. But, because the planes had fallen far beyond the view of the official observers, they could not be counted. For his services with the escadrille Lufbery was awarded decorations by both the French and British governments.

America's first ace received the rank of major when he transferred to the Air Service. He was sent to Issoudun, south of Paris, where the United States had set up a large aviation instruction center. At Issoudun American pilots were given advanced training in the latest French and English planes.

Instead of making Lufbery an instructor, a job he was well qualified to fill, the Air Service assigned the veteran combat pilot to an office job. The only office Lufbery wanted to sit in was the cockpit of a speedy Nieuport. He protested that he would be much more useful in the air teaching the new American fliers the things he had learned in his many aerial battles with the enemy. Being a fighter pilot was a dangerous business. The new men needed all the help they could get.

Lufbery's arguments made a great deal of sense. He was soon assigned to help with the training of the newly organized 94th and 95th Pursuit Squadrons.

In the beginning the two squadrons were equipped with Nieuports that lacked machine guns. This was a serious deficiency. Not only was it difficult to teach fighter tactics to an inexperienced pilot in a plane without a gun; it was also risky. A pilot in an unarmed plane was helpless if he met enemy aircraft.

Nevertheless, Lufbery taught his men the combat methods he had found most effective. He took them into the air to get them accustomed to spotting enemy aircraft. They had to learn not to focus on any one point but to gaze around. Then they would see anything within their field of vision. The fledgling aviators actually flew some patrols in their unarmed planes.

On April 13, 1918, the 94th Pursuit Squadron, which by then had received its guns, became the first unit of the United States Air Service ready for combat in France. The squadron was stationed at Toul, then a comparatively quiet sector, but the very next day its pilots downed two enemy aircraft. During the next few weeks the pilots of the 94th, who were joined at Toul by the 95th Pursuit Squadron, flew patrols and acquired some of the experience they needed before moving closer to the lines. On the morning of May 19, a Sunday, many of them witnessed a battle they would never forget.

At 10:00 A.M. the 94th received a telephoned report of a German reconnaissance plane heading for Toul. The squadron kept a pilot on alert, ready to take off at once in such an emergency. Within minutes he was in the air.

As the enemy plane flew toward Toul, anti-aircraft batteries kept it under a steady barrage of gunfire. Suddenly the intruder went into a spin. The anti-aircraft guns stopped firing. The gunners were sure they had downed the plane. But at 200 feet the German pilot leveled off and began to streak away with the plane from the 94th in pursuit.

Raoul Lufbery, watching from the edge of the airfield, saw that the German was going to get away. He rushed to the hangars where the planes were parked. His own Nieuport was out of commission, but there was one standing near by ready to go. He jumped in. Using every bit of power the rotary engine could deliver, he tore after the departing German two-seater. As he approached his target, Lufbery fired several short bursts. Then his gun seemed to jam. He swerved away and spectators on the ground could see him work on his gun. Then the jam cleared and he was after the enemy once more. When he was quite close he fired several times, but his bullets seemed to have little effect.

Suddenly the horrified watchers on the ground saw the Nieuport falter. Its cockpit became a mass of flames. Desperately Lufbery tried to maneuver his ship to blow the flames away, but the fire was everywhere. The German gunner had hit the gas tank, which was located next to the pilot's seat.

The next moment the gallant flier's body was plunging headlong through the air. It crashed in a garden within sight of the Toul airfield.

The ace of the *Escadrille Lafayette* was buried the next day in a small cemetery near the airfield. As his body was lowered into its grave, his fellow pilots flew slowly above, dropping flowers as a last tribute to their fallen comrade.

EDWARD MANNOCK, BRITAIN'S LEADING ACE

When World War I began, the man who was to become Britain's leading ace was in Turkey. Edward Mannock had gone there in January, 1914, to work for a British-controlled telephone company. In October, 1914, Turkey entered the war as a partner of Germany and Austria-Hungary. Because Great Britain was fighting on the other side, all Englishmen in Turkey were regarded as enemies of that country. Many of them, including Edward Mannock, were placed in prison camps.

Even before he fell into the hands of the Turks, Mannock's life had not been easy. He grew up in a poor family of five children. When he was twelve, his father disappeared and life became very difficult. The family was living in the cathedral town of Canterbury at the time. Edward's mother and his two older brothers earned what money they could, but it

wasn't enough. Edward had to leave school and go
to work. He started out as a delivery boy, carrying
groceries for the housewives of Canterbury. Then
he found a job in a barber shop. Next he became a
telephone linesman and this eventually led to his
going to Turkey, where there were good jobs for
experienced telephone men.

Mannock remained a prisoner in Turkey until
April, 1915. Then, because he was twenty-seven years
old, in poor health, and having trouble with his eyes,
the Turks sent him back to England. No doubt
Turkish officials were convinced that such a wreck
of a man would be of little help to the British war
effort. They were wrong. Edward Mannock was to
shoot down no less than seventy-three enemy planes,
enough to make several combat squadrons.

Before leaving home to work in Turkey, Mannock
had belonged to a medical corps unit of the British
army. One of the first things he did when he returned
to England was rejoin his old unit. After some months
in the medical corps he decided he would rather be
a sapper. In World War I a sapper was a member of
an engineering unit whose job was to dig tunnels
beneath the enemy's lines. Dynamite was then placed
in the tunnel to blow up the unsuspecting enemy.
This seemed a good idea to Edward Mannock, who
had developed an intense dislike for the Germans. He
told a friend: "I intend to become a tunneling officer
and blow 'em up."

It was about this time—the summer of 1916—that the aerial exploits of Albert Ball were beginning to fill the pages of the newspapers and magazines in Great Britain. Fierce battles were raging on the Somme front, where the British had attacked German positions. Every day Ball was aloft in his Nieuport, searching the skies for enemy planes, and the British press reported his activities in detail.

Edward Mannock read the reports with a great deal of interest. Although he was some years older than Ball, Mannock began to make a personal hero of the British ace. The work of a sapper seemed dull indeed compared with what Ball was doing in France. Mannock applied for a transfer to the Royal Flying Corps.

There were several reasons why this application was not likely to be accepted. For one thing, Mannock was now twenty-nine years old. Most student pilots started out at a considerably younger age. Even more serious, he suffered from astigmatism in his left eye. Whatever he saw with that eye was blurred. The Royal Flying Corps insisted upon perfect vision. Mannock knew the odds were against his being accepted, but he was determined to become a flier.

Somehow he managed to pass the eye examination, which was his greatest problem. There is still speculation about how he did it. Some say he memorized the eye chart. Others claim he must have used his good eye for both parts of the examination. At any rate, his transfer to the Royal Flying Corps was approved in August, 1916.

The happy pilot-to-be wrote in his diary: "When the Adjutant sent for me today and informed me of my transfer to the Royal Flying Corps, I could have kissed him although he has the most repulsive mug of any man I have ever met."

Away he went, first to ground school and then to Hendon, where Albert Ball had taken his flying lessons. By the end of November, Edward Mannock had his pilot's certificate. Advanced training was next. At Joyce Green, where Mannock was sent for his advanced work, his instructor was Captain James McCudden. Like Mannock, McCudden was to become one of Britain's leading aces. At Joyce Green the two fliers became good friends.

When he finished his training, Mannock joined No. 40 Squadron in France, arriving there early in April, 1917. For the Royal Flying Corps that month was "Bloody April." Losses of men and aircraft were higher in April, 1917, than in any other month of the entire war.

The German air force had started 1917 with a superior new fighter, the Albatros D. III. It took off quickly and could climb to 9,800 feet in twelve minutes. At an altitude of 3,280 feet it traveled at a speedy 109 miles an hour. The D. III carried two deadly Spandau machine guns. Its one defect was a tendency to stay in a dive once a pilot pointed its nose downward. Even so, in April of 1917, neither the French nor the British had a plane to equal the Albatros D. III.

German pilots in the D. III were able to fly over the British lines almost at will. But when British pilots in their slower planes ventured over the German lines, many of them were shot down. Seventy-five British planes, carrying 105 men, were lost between April 4 and April 8. On April 6 alone, forty-four planes went down.

That was the situation that greeted Edward Mannock when he reported to No. 40 Squadron. For several weeks he did little to improve it. Because Great Britain was producing only limited numbers of fighter aircraft, some of her squadrons were equipped with French planes. Number 40 Squadron flew the Nieuport 17. Mannock spent many hours learning to fly the Nieuport and more hours in the gunnery pits trying out his gun. Accurate shooting was difficult for him because of his bad left eye, but hours of practice made him a better-than-average shot.

As the days went by and Mannock seemed to do more practicing than fighting, his squadron mates began to wonder if he would ever make a good combat pilot. Most of them thought he was being overly cautious. Some thought he might be a coward. Apparently oblivious of what was being said about him, Mannock continued his self-imposed training program. He knew that, because of his poor eyesight,

Edward "Mickey" Mannock

he would have to work extra hard to succeed as a fighter pilot.

Mannock had been with No. 40 Squadron for a month before he engaged in his first successful combat. On May 7, 1917, he shot down an observa-

A squadron of Nieuport 17s at a British base in France.

tion balloon. Balloons were difficult and dangerous targets. Because they were usually surrounded by a ring of anti-aircraft guns, a pilot had to be an expert flier and a good shot to knock one down.

Mannock's feat improved his standing in the squadron, but another month passed before he was successful in combat again. The second victim was a German two-seater. Shortly after this victory he went on leave.

When Mannock returned to No. 40 Squadron in July, 1917, his luck semed to change. Or perhaps the long hours he had spent learning to use his plane and gun were beginning to bring results. .At any rate, he began to shoot down enemy planes with a regularity that astounded his fellow pilots, especially those who had predicted he would never turn into a fighter. Before the month was over, he had been promoted to the rank of captain and made a flight commander.

Leading a flight turned out to be the thing Mannock did best of all. He was unequaled in the way he could plan a patrol, prepare his men for every possible enemy action, and watch over them while they were in the air.

As a flight commander, Mannock's first concern was the safety of the men who flew with him. He spent a great deal of time with each new pilot. He took them up on practice flights and on patrols over safe areas. He taught them how to fly in formation, the best way to spot enemy planes, and the safest method of shooting them down. More than once he withdrew after hitting a German plane so that a new man could finish it off. And he would see to it that the young pilot got the credit for the kill. In this way he helped his new pilots over their first difficult weeks of combat. It gave them the confidence that could mean the difference between life and death in aerial warfare.

In spite of all the time he devoted to training his men, Mannock was able to add to his own list of victories. These increased rapidly after December, 1917, for in that month No. 40 Squadron began to fly a new plane, the S.E. 5 (Scouting Experimental). A product of the British Royal Aircraft Factory, the small and maneuverable S.E. 5 was faster than the Nieuport 17. Mannock used the additional speed to good advantage in attacking the enemy. When he returned to England early in January to assist in the training of new combat pilots, his score stood at twenty-three.

During Mannock's stay at the front, the war came a great deal closer to the British people. On May 25, '917, German Gotha bombers flew over the English coast dropping bombs that killed ninety-five people and injured 192. The British had already been bombed—during the Zeppelin raids in 1915 and 1916—but the big four-motored dirigibles had failed to arouse the feeling of terror produced by the Gothas. Dire predictions that the Zeppelins would destroy the cities of England and France never materialized. Instead the slow-moving, flammable Zeppelins proved no match for defending airplanes armed with explosive bullets.

Sporadic Zeppelin raids continued into the early months of 1917, but they did little damage. In all the Zeppelins dropped 5,806 bombs and killed 557 people.

The Gothas were a more formidable enemy, harder to destroy and capable of causing greater destruction. On June 13, 1917, twenty Gothas dropped more than four tons of bombs on London, killing 162, injuring 432, and inflicting widespread damage on the city. More raids followed.

Improved defenses forced the Gothas to attack under the protection of darkness, but the British found the night raids even more terrible. In retalia-

(Above) German Zeppelin L-2, completed in 1915, departs for her first combat mission. Such Zeppelins were basically gasbags supported by a light framework. (Below) A French plane attacks a German Zeppelin somewhere above the battlefront.

tion, they organized a special air force to bomb German cities. Called the Independent Air Force, it dropped 500 tons of bombs on Germany during the last five months of the war. Neither side, however, was able to seriously disrupt the other's war effort.

In spite of the bombing attacks, Edward Mannock found it hard to adjust to the quiet and inactivity of life in England. Like Albert Ball before him, he submitted numerous requests to be returned to the fighting in France. He even threatened to go back to France without official permission.

Finally he received orders sending him to No. 74 Squadron, then training for combat. Mannock was to be one of the flight commanders. Happy to be returning to flying once more, he began to teach his pilots

The Gotha bomber, a formidable enemy.

how to handle the S.E. 5 with skill and precision. Late in March he took them to France.

Earlier that month the Germans had launched their big spring offensive. With the United States about to enter the conflict, the German generals realized that, if they didn't win the war soon, they weren't going to win it at all. After a five-hour artillery bombardment, they sent planes to attack the British troops on the Somme front. The soldiers on the ground had already been attacked, or strafed, by airplanes. But previous attacks had been carried out by just a few planes at a time. Now the Germans used a great many airplanes in a carefully planned attack. They wrought havoc among the British troops. Before the battle was over, the German armies had advanced forty-one miles. The Allies feared that this time the enemy couldn't be stopped. And another German advance in early April seemed to confirm this fear. It looked very much as if Germany, already victorious on the Eastern Front, would win in the West, too.

The Allies reacted to their desperate situation by combining their separate army commands into one under the direction of French Marshal Ferdinand Foch. They also urged the United States to send troops to France as quickly as possible. In May the Germans attacked again and advanced to the Marne River.

While the opposing armies struggled on the ground, the Allied and German air forces fought above the battlefields. It was a busy time for airmen, especially for Edward Mannock. He flew almost every day and, in the three months he spent with No. 74 Squadron, shot down thirty-six enemy ships. He seemed to be able to find the weak point of each plane he met in combat.

In June of 1918 Mannock was promoted to the rank of major. Shortly afterward he was given a squadron of his own to command—No. 85. Once more he set about teaching less experienced fliers all he had learned about the art of aerial fighting. He led his squadron with great skill and daring. And he continued to take a special interest in the new men who were just starting out as combat pilots.

At dawn on July 26, 1918, Mannock headed for the German lines with another new and untried pilot, D. C. Inglis. For a while they flew back and forth in their S.E. 5s with Mannock leading and Inglis under orders to stay close on his tail. Suddenly Mannock made a quick turn and started to climb. Then there was another quick turn followed by a dive. Mannock had spotted a German two-seater. He fired a burst as he passed the enemy ship, then moved off to make way for Inglis, who was coming up behind him. Inglis fired and hit the two-seater's fuel tank. The enemy plane went down in flames. Inglis was no longer an untried pilot; he had scored his first victory.

The two Englishmen circled until the two-seater hit the ground. Then they started for home with Inglis still flying behind Mannock. They had dropped fairly low when Inglis noticed that Mannock was side-slipping. Then he saw a flame burst from the airplane ahead. The flame grew bigger and Mannock's S.E. 5 went out of control. It was still burning when it hit the ground.

Inglis circled the spot where his commander had crashed, but he saw no signs of life. The German anti-aircraft gunners who had hit Mannock's fuel tank were now zeroing in on Inglis. He had to leave.

Edward Mannock had lost his life helping another man to become a good fighter pilot. Although Mannock's seventy-three victories made him Britain's leading ace, his greatest contribution to his country's war effort may have been the many young fliers he turned into skillful aerial warriors at a time when they were badly needed.

WILLY COPPENS, FIGHTER FOR BELGIUM

It was just a few minutes before ten o'clock on the morning of February 18, 1918. The roof tops of Brussels, the capital city of Belgium, shone in the sunlight. A solitary fighter plane appeared in the sky to the south of the city and flew steadily toward it. The plane was painted blue. On its wing tips were the tricolor circles of the Belgian air force, now based in France.

No Belgian plane had flown over Brussels for many months. Early in the war the city had been captured by the Germans, who made it one of the most heavily defended places in Europe. Anti-aircraft guns sur rounded the city to shoot down any Allied plane that dared approach it.

Who was this daring pilot flying alone over enemy territory? His name was Willy Coppens, and he was one of the best fliers in the Belgian air force.

Willy Coppens

For weeks Willy had been thinking about making a trip to Brussels. His parents lived there. Although he didn't hope to see them, he thought all the citizens of Brussels would be cheered at the sight of one of their own planes defying the Germans.

At first his senior officers refused to let Willy go, insisting that no plane could get past the anti-aircraft guns. But Willy went on planning. He thought he could do it, and at last he received permission to try.

Luck was with him from the beginning. As he passed over the German lines, two French Spads happened to pass beneath him. The German anti-aircraft gunners fired at the French planes while Willy flew on unnoticed. He reached the city of Bruge and then followed the railroad to Brussels. He saw only one German plane on the way, and it dived steeply away from him.

Once he was over Brussels, Willy brought his plane down low. The familiar buildings stood out clearly in the sunlight. He saw the streets along which he had walked so many times. There was *la rue des Champs Elysées*. His street! As he passed a tall white house with a red roof, he flew still lower. It was his parents' home.

A man in a brown overcoat ran out of the house and stood looking up at the low-flying plane. Could that be his father? Willy couldn't tell for sure, but the man had seen the tricolor circles on the wings of the blue plane. The whole neighborhood could see that one of their own fighters was flying over the capital.

Willy turned and flew back over the tall white house for one more look. This time he saw two women standing at a window. One of them might be his mother. If only he could see more clearly.

Willy reluctantly turned his plane away. If he stayed any longer, the Germans might start firing. He didn't want any of the townspeople to be injured. Keeping his plane low, so that the Germans couldn't spot him, he flew back toward the lines. He had been over Brussels just thirteen minutes. What a lucky thirteen minutes it had been!

Willy returned to his airfield at Les Moeres near the French border in time for a late breakfast. His fellow pilots were eager to hear what had happened.

"What about the anti-aircraft guns?" they asked.

"How did Brussels look?"

"Were there many German planes about?"

Willy answered their questions until his commanding officer sent for him. A short time later he left the headquarters building with his commander's congratulations ringing in his ears.

The daring flight to Brussels was an example of the kind of fighting Willy Coppens believed in.

"You must take the war to the enemy," he said. "You must attack and go on attacking all the time."

Willy began his military career in 1912 at the age of twenty. Like most young Belgians he had to serve in the army before starting his civilian career. The regiment he joined was the 2nd Grenadiers.

When Germany invaded Belgium on August 4, 1914, the outnumbered Belgian army put up a gallant, but hopeless fight. One by one the cities of Belgium were captured until the enemy occupied all the country except a part of Flanders in the southwest. As the Belgian army retreated, it continued to fight the advancing Germans. The small Belgian air force (it was called the *Compagnie des Aviateurs*) withdrew with the army. In the fall of 1914 Belgian aviators

Coppens (center) with a group of Belgian officers.

were flying reconnaissance and bombing missions from an airfield at St. Pol in France. In the beginning they sometimes had to use borrowed equipment because they had lost much of their own to the invaders. Gradually the Belgians acquired new airplanes, and also began to recruit and train men to fly them.

Willy Coppens transferred to the air force at this time. When he left the Grenadiers, the new Belgian training school wasn't quite ready to begin teaching pilots. So Willy, along with thirty-nine other young Belgians, went to England at his own expense to learn to fly at a civilian flying school.

Coppens had to borrow money to pay for his two months of flying lessons. The school he attended at Hendon was one of a number of civilian flying schools that were operating in England. Some of them didn't have enough planes and instructors to do a good job of teaching a beginning pilot to fly. Willy's school was one of these. In looking back on his early training he recalled: "When we left Hendon, we didn't even know that one had to land head to the wind."

From Hendon he went to the school operated by the Belgian air force at Etampes, France, for more training. There he learned to fly the Farman observation plane. The Farmans at the school were old models no longer considered good enough for combat. This didn't discourage Willy Coppens. He liked to fly.

A Maurice Farman in flight. These two-seat reconnaissance planes were often used in training missions.

By July, 1916, Coppens had flown enough hours to pass the pilot's examination. He was ready to go to the front and help the Belgian army fight the enemy, but no assignment came. France and England supplied the aircraft used by the Belgians, and sometimes planes were not available. Finally Coppens reported to a newly organized squadron equipped with Farmans and B.E. 2s. Both were old, slow biplanes used for reconnaissance and occasionally for bombing missions. Coppens was disappointed. He had hoped to fly something faster when he became a full-fledged pilot.

While flying in a B.E. 2, the future Belgian ace came under enemy fire for the first time. In a B.E. 2 the observer rode in the front seat with a machine gun. The pilot was in the rear seat. Willy's B.E. 2 came through the attack with only minor damage, but the young Belgian was more convinced than ever that it was an inferior airplane.

Shortly afterward his squadron received some Sopwith 1½ Strutters, British two-seaters so named because of the unusual "W" shape of their center-section wing supports, or struts. The observer rode in the rear seat with the fuel tank between him and the pilot in the front seat. When the Belgian fliers saw the dangerous location of the fuel tank, they decided that the designer of the plane must have been a German.

Coppens was flying in a Sopwith the day he had his first real air fight. While on patrol over Hout-

Charles Nungesser, another famous French ace. The eerie insignia on the plane was Nungesser's personal symbol throughout the war. Here it appears on a Morane-Saulnier, a plane the celebrated French ace flew when no Nieuports were available.

hulst Forest near the front lines, he saw four German fighters climbing toward him. He and his observer both watched the approaching planes carefully. They wanted to be ready for the attack when it came.

Suddenly there was a *rat-tat-tat* of machine-gun fire. Four other enemy fighters had crept up unseen. Coppens quickly swung to the right and avoided the worst of the barrage.

A short while before this, the Belgian had met the famous French ace, Charles Nungesser, who had given him some advice on aerial fighting. The Frenchman had pointed out that a two-seater airplane, under attack by a faster single-seater, should turn steeply whenever the single-seater dived upon it. The single-seater could only fire straight ahead. By twisting and turning, the two-seater could avoid getting hit. At the same time, its observer with his movable gun had a good chance of downing the attacking plane.

"I remembered this piece of advice," Coppens said, "and kept continuously turning, first one way and then the other, rarely coming back for more than a second onto an even keel."

Nungesser may well have saved the two Belgians' lives because all four of the enemy planes were attacking. Willy himself had no machine gun, but his observer returned the Germans' fire. The Sopwith was hit thirty-two times before the two Belgians managed to escape.

Both men received much praise for bringing the badly damaged plane back. But Willy simply said, "Of course I had to bring it back. I needed it to take me home."

In July, 1917, Coppens was transferred to the Belgian airfield at Les Moeres. When he discovered that his new squadron flew the famous single-seat Nieuport, he was overjoyed. Soon he was patrolling the battlefields, first in a Nieuport and then in a Hanriot, another French plane. The Hanriot, a small maneuverable fighter, provided excellent visibility for the pilot. But weeks passed and Coppens failed to knock down a single enemy plane.

Coppens, a skillful flier, constantly had trouble with the Hanriot's single gun. More than once, when he had the enemy lined up in his sights, his gun would not fire a shot. During this period of disappointment, Coppens made his flight over Brussels. His daring excursion may have done little for the war effort, but it did much to restore Willy's fighting spirit. He began to think about shooting down balloons. No Belgian aviator had shot one down, although several had tried.

German balloon observers had been able to gather a great deal of valuable information about Allied troop movements along the front. The sharp-eyed observers swung in baskets below their gasbags two to five miles from the lines and watched for signs of enemy activity. The stationary balloonist was able to do a more careful job than an observer in a moving plane. The information he gathered was telephoned to the ground at once. A message such as—"A large truck convoy moving up to the front; map sector 12, approaching coordinates north 123 and west 17"— would bring immediate action from German artillery. Chances were that the convoy would never reach its destination.

When Allied artillery went into action, the enemy balloonist was able to locate its source and direct the fire of German guns to knock it out. Of course such valuable sources of military intelligence as the observation balloons were extremely well protected by anti-aircraft guns. In addition, the balloons could be pulled down at the approach of an enemy plane. A successful attack on one of the German balloons was

A captured German observation balloon.

considered both difficult and extremely dangerous.

A month after his flight to Brussels, Coppens volunteered to attack an enemy observation balloon behind the lines at Bovekerke, near the French–Belgian border. This balloon had directed the enemy fire that forced a Belgian cavalry division to retreat. The division was badly needed at the front, so the balloon at Bovekerke had to be destroyed.

The balloon usually floated at an altitude of about 3,000 feet. In order to avoid the many anti-aircraft guns guarding it, Coppens climbed to 7,500 feet. Then he dived on the balloon at full speed.

The anti-aircraft guns began to fire, and the ground crew started to pull in the balloon. Coppens continued his dive until he was near enough to use his Vickers gun. But even at close range he could not set the balloon afire. At last he was forced to break off. Before he left he put his Hanriot into a beautiful loop, which must have surprised the German gunners shooting at him. Then he headed for home.

The balloon at Bovekerkc had not been destroyed, but it had provided some valuable information. Coppens was convinced that he had failed because he hadn't used the right ammunition. But what sort of ammunition would be right? Perhaps some type of incendiary bullet.

Willy went to the commander of a nearby British airfield and asked for a few incendiary bullets. He used them against another balloon, but with no better luck than before. It failed to catch fire.

Next Coppens arranged to try some French ammunition. Because the supply was limited, he planned to use no more than four of the incendiary bullets and to come within 150 feet of his target before using his gun.

This time the balloon was at Zarren near the border. Coppens dived down upon it as he had done before. As he came zooming through the anti-aircraft fire, he saw a parachute open. The observer had jumped from the balloon.

Both German and Allied balloonmen used parachutes, although airmen did not. The heavy, cumbersome parachutes were attached to the balloon rigging. When an observer jumped, his weight detached the chute and pulled the ripcord. (Late in the war, the Germans developed a more compact parachute that could be used in a plane.)

The observer had almost reached the ground when Coppens decided his plane was close enough for him to shoot at the balloon. He had waited so long that he almost rammed it. Quickly pulling around, he looked back to see it burst into flames. He had been successful!

Coppens returned to the airfield. Dipping into his precious supply of incendiary bullets, he added four more of them to his regular ammunition and set off again. This time he headed for a balloon over nearby Houthulst Forest. Following the procedure he had worked out, he came diving down on the gasbag. Before long it too was on fire.

After that day, much to the delight of the Belgian soldiers in the trenches, Coppens went after balloons as fast as the Germans put them up. Other pilots adopted his method of dealing with balloons, but Willy was the recognized expert. Many stories were told of his skill as a balloon destroyer. Once he actually landed on top of a balloon.

Coppens had flown in very close in order to fire at the balloon. As he crossed above it, the balloon suddenly shot up. The wheels of Willy's Hanriot struck the gasbag. As the balloon began to sink under the weight of the plane, Coppens did the thing that probably saved his life. He turned off his engine. This kept the propeller from getting smashed or entangled with the gasbag. The plane slithered across the surface of the balloon and off the edge. When he

A drawing of Coppens' plane accidentally landing on top of a German observation balloon.

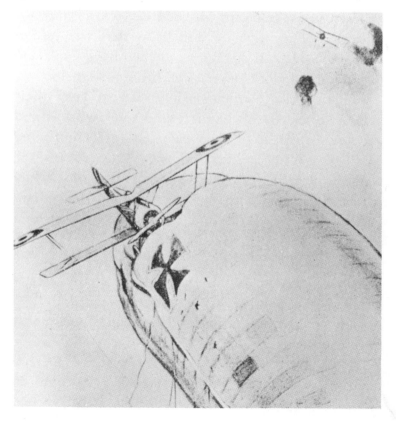

was clear, Coppens started his engine. The balloon fell to earth and burst into flames.

Not all Coppens' time was spent in knocking down balloons, however. He took part in the regular fighter patrols of his squadron. And here too his luck changed. He shot down so many enemy planes that the Germans began to call his blue Hanriot the "Blue Devil."

Because he was destroying so many planes and balloons, the Germans decided to set a trap for Coppens. They put up a balloon that was loaded with explosives. If he hit it, the resulting explosion would take care of Coppens and his blue Hanriot.

Although the Germans tried hard to keep their plan a secret, the Belgians found out about it and planned a surprise of their own. By carefully timing his flight, Willy arrived on the scene just as the Germans started to raise their special balloon. When it was only halfway up, he let go with his incendiary bullets. There was a loud explosion. The balloon turned into a huge fireball and fell to the ground. Many of the Germans who had gathered to watch the destruction of the "Blue Devil" were unable to get away in time. Although Coppens had turned away as quickly as he could, his plane bounced around as if it were a feather.

On October 14, 1918, Coppens received an important assignment. A balloon at Thourout, in German-occupied southwestern Belgium, had located

Allied artillery units and was directing enemy gun-fire at them. The Allies, who were attacking German positions in Belgium, needed the help of the beleaguered artillerymen.

When Coppens arrived at Thourout, he found an enemy balloon floating approximately 2,000 feet above the ground. He made his usual steep dive on the target, but before he was close enough to fire, his plane was rocked by a sharp explosion. The blue Hanriot went into a spin. Willy's left leg had been shattered by shrapnel. He was headed for a crash landing in enemy territory.

In spite of his great pain, Coppens managed to get his good foot back on the rudder bar. With considerable effort he straightened his plane and headed in the direction of home.

When he could no longer hear the German guns, he began watching for a place to land. He was losing a great deal of blood and rapidly becoming too weak to fly. He saw a small field alongside which there was a road. If he landed there, perhaps someone would see him and come to his aid.

Coppens had chosen well. Belgian troops from a nearby camp came running to pull him from his damaged plane. He was rushed to the nearest hospital. His leg was so badly wounded that it had to be amputated.

The war had ended for Willy Coppens. But by scoring thirty-seven victories over German planes and balloons, Belgium's leading ace had proved the soundness of his own advice: "You must take the war to the enemy. You must attack and go on attacking all the time."

DAVE INGALLS, NAVY ACE

The United States Navy acquired its first airplanes—a Wright and a Curtiss land plane and a Curtiss amphibian—in 1911. Three Navy men were trained as pilots by the Wright and Curtiss companies and the planes became scouts for the fleet. Although the scouting experiment proved a success, the Navy's air arm grew very slowly. Six years later, in 1917, the Navy had only twenty-one planes and barely enough pilots and mechanics to keep them in the air.

When the United States entered the war in April, 1917, the Navy needed far more than twenty-one planes to carry out just one of its assignments—patrolling the country's coasts. Hundreds of new planes were ordered and pilot-training schools were filled to capacity. But an expansion program begun in 1917 would not produce results until 1918, or later. In the meantime the Navy was badly in need of both experienced aviators and battle-worthy airplanes.

Help came from an unexpected source—a group of Yale University students who had learned to fly seaplanes. The young men had become interested in aviation after reading about the exploits of Albert Ball, Georges Guynemer, the members of the *Escadrille Américaine,* and other air heroes. They decided that they, too, wanted to serve their country as aviators.

Fortunately, the twelve members of the group had wealthy parents and influential friends, because both were needed to carry out their ambitious plans. They intended to take over a flying school on Long Island Sound along with a flying boat and an instructor. Relatives gave them two more flying boats and during the 1916 summer vacation, three of the students soloed.

Before the boys returned to Yale in the fall, the Navy conducted a series of practice exercises near their flying school. There were no Navy planes in the area, so the Yale men were asked to see if they could locate a mine field and a group of destroyers from the air. Pleased to show what they could do, the student pilots located them both.

When classes resumed at Yale, flying lessons continued on a part-time basis. There were also occasional invitations to assist the Navy—such as flying over submarines to see if they could be spotted from the air.

H-12 type seaplane used for training in Florida.

The young aviators formally organized the Yale Aero Club that fall. The Club proved so popular that a Second Unit followed, and then a Third Unit. In the meantime, as war with Germany appeared more and more inevitable, the members of the original Aero Club, or the First Unit, offered to begin training for active Navy duty. Their offer was refused because the Navy could not take over a civilian group. Late in March, 1917, however, twenty-eight young men from the Yale Aero Club's First Unit joined the Naval Reserve. They then left school and went to Palm Beach, Florida, to continue their privately financed training program.

The First Yale Unit spent two months at Palm Beach and then moved to Huntington, New York, to finish training. By this time the country was at war, and aviation officers were needed at naval stations in the United States and overseas. As members of the Naval Reserve, the former Yale students were ordered to active duty as soon as they completed training. Some of them reported to naval stations in the United States; the rest were sent to France.

Dave Ingalls was one of those whose orders said "France." A native of Cleveland, Ohio, he had joined the Aero Club during his freshman year at Yale. In September, 1917, with six other former Yale students, he sailed for France. Their destination was the American naval aviation station at Moutchic, which operated as a school for newly arrived pilots.

Even though the members of the First Yale Unit had left the United States as trained aviators, they received more training after reporting at Moutchic. And in December Ingalls was sent to still another school—at Gosport in England.

Eager as he was to join a combat unit, Ingalls enjoyed his stay at Gosport because he learned to fly the Sopwith Camel. The Sopwith Camel was one of the Allies' fastest and most maneuverable planes. Its 130 horsepower Clerget engine could do 115 miles per hour. The young American liked the way the plane made quick turns and steep dives, and the way

David S. Ingalls

it could climb almost straight up. Before he left Gosport, Ingalls had spent hours zooming through the English skies practicing slow rolls and dives.

After Gosport came still another school, this time in Scotland. Finally, in March, 1918, his training was completed. Ensign David Ingalls returned to France. He arrived at the American naval air station at Dunkirk just as the Germans began their big spring offensive. When the Americans, not yet engaged in a mission of their own, offered their services to the hard-pressed British, Ingalls and three others were "borrowed" by No. 213 Squadron of the Royal Air Force. No. 213 Squadron was assigned to sea patrol.

Ingalls would have preferred duty with a fighter squadron, but with No. 213 he did get a chance to fly Camels again. In a swift Camel he flew up and down the coast, looking for the enemy's aerial patrols, supply ships, and submarines.

The prime target of No. 213's sea patrols was the German submarine fleet which prowled the seas around Great Britain and France, looking for Allied troop and supply ships. A patrolling plane could spot a submarine near the surface. The wake left by a diving submarine was plainly visible from the air. Once it sighted a submarine, the patrolling plane would attempt to hit it with bombs, a difficult feat. The patrols were reasonably effective, but they required hours of tedious flying.

The German advance was checked after a month of bitter fighting, and the American airmen returned to their own station at Dunkirk. There they found that airplanes and other equipment were still in very short supply. Nevertheless, the Americans tried to maintain sea patrols in their assigned area. Dave Ingalls, chafing at the lack of activity, flew whenever a plane was available, but he missed the fine equipment of the British No. 213 Squadron. Most of all he missed flying in the speedy Camel.

Ingalls knew that some Americans had continued to fly with British squadrons. He asked to be reassigned to No. 213, and his request was granted. No. 213 Squadron no longer engaged exclusively in sea patrols,

During World War I the Sopwith Camel, one of the most formidable of British fighting scouts, destroyed more enemy aircraft than any other single type of Allied plane.

but it still used the Camel. So Dave became a Camel pilot once more.

He went on several patrols with other members of No. 213 Squadron without seeing a single German fighter or observation plane. Dave wanted action. If he went out alone he might surprise a Fokker. He asked his commander for permission to patrol by himself.

Although solo flying was discouraged, the young American naval pilot's wish was granted. Perhaps his commanding officer thought a solo flight would teach Dave the value of teamwork in tracking down the enemy.

The blue sky was filled with fleecy white clouds as Dave approached the Belgian border. A deft touch on the stick and a slight pressure on the rudder guided his Camel through the cold air as he looked in vain for a German ship. For an hour he flew up and down; there wasn't another plane in the sky. Even the usually busy anti-aircraft guns seemed to be taking a holiday.

Reluctantly Dave decided to head for home. As he put his Camel on its left wing to bank around, he looked over his shoulder. Three Fokkers were roaring down at him from a patch of cloud! That was more than he had bargained for. Even a veteran pilot would have been in trouble.

The Fokkers were on top of him in a flash. Their tracers tore away at the fabric of his wings and smacked against the fuselage. Dave kicked his rudder from right to left in an effort to avoid the stream of bullets.

Then one of the Fokkers came screaming straight at him with guns blazing. Just in time the naval pilot slammed on full left rudder and swung over. The Fokker overshot him. Now it was Ingalls' turn. As the Fokker reappeared in front of him, he let go with both his guns.

The other two Fokkers came to the rescue. Once

more Dave was forced to twist and dodge as bullets ripped into his plane. The battle raged back and forth across the sky as Dave tried in vain to break away.

Suddenly the chatter of gunfire stopped. Expecting a renewed attack from another direction, Ingalls turned his Camel and looked around. The three Fokkers were heading back toward their own lines. Perhaps they had run out of ammunition, or perhaps they had just decided to go home.

The American was more than happy to see them go. Although he had held off the three planes, his Camel had been shot full of holes. He decided his commander was right—fighting in the air was not a one-man job. It required teamwork.

One day, while on a patrol over the German trenches, Ingalls became separated from his flight during a dive through a layer of clouds. As he searched for his companions, he saw something move below him. It was a two-seated Rumpler, painted red, with the black cross of Germany on its wing tips. Dave put his plane into a dive.

In the rear seat of the Rumpler rode an observer with a Parabellum machine gun pointed out over the tail. The German immediately opened fire on Dave's Camel. Ingalls could see that he had little to fear from the marksmanship of this gunner.

The American held his fire, moving in closer and closer. At 100 yards he pressed his triggers. The

German plane maneuvered violently. Then the pilot put it into a steep dive toward the trenches.

This was an old trick and Dave had been warned to watch out for it. The German pilot was trying to force the faster Camel to dive into the ground. Dave waited until the German pulled out of his dive and began to climb. Then he went after him.

At 5,000 feet they leveled off and exchanged fire. A row of small black holes appeared in the Camel's cowling. Dave had flown within range of the enemy observer's gun. He decided that he had better make use of the Camel's speed. He dived again at the Rumpler. As he closed in, he fired. The observer did not fire back. One of Dave's shots had silenced him.

A flickering finger of flame appeared over the Rumpler's gas tank. The two-seater turned over and went streaking earthward leaving a trail of black smoke behind it.

David Ingalls of the United States Navy had shot down his first plane.

Just two days later he flew on a mission to Varsenaere, twenty miles behind the enemy lines in Belgium. The Germans had built up a huge airfield at Varsenaere. Many of the Fokkers that rose to do battle with the English airmen came from there. And bombers based at Varsenaere were out almost every night bringing destruction to the surrounding area. The British fliers were going to give them a taste of their own medicine.

The attack was carefully planned. Camels and DeHavilland 9 bombers took off at dawn and headed for Belgium. It was a cloudy morning, but they flew above the clouds in the sunshine. Not an enemy plane was in sight.

Finally the leader waggled his wings, the signal for a descent through the clouds. They went down in a tight V formation.

The Germans had installed a ring of anti-aircraft guns to protect their airfield. As soon as the English planes broke through the clouds, the guns began to chatter. Fire sparkled on all sides of the attacking ships. Holes appeared in wings and fuselages, but no one turned back.

The Camels and D.H. 9s were over the airfield before the Germans could get their planes into the air. The rows of Fokkers lined up on the field made a good target. Soon the noise of machine guns was added to the rattle of the anti-aircraft barrage as a series of well-placed shots set the Fokkers ablaze.

Dave Ingalls had a special assignment—to destroy some machine shops located behind the hangars. With four 20-pound bombs in his racks, he swung over a burning hangar and let the bombs go whistling down toward a group of repair shops. He heard the bombs explode as they struck. The target disappeared in a cloud of smoke, and Dave turned for home through a hail of bullets. The German gunners were still on the job.

After the successful raid on Varsenaere the young American was made a flight commander. Now he would be leading less experienced pilots on missions against the enemy.

On one of his first missions in his new capacity, he led a flight of five Camels to Utkerke, where they attacked another German airfield. After the field had been bombed, Ingalls made a last circuit to survey the damage. Then he hurried off to rejoin his flight.

He had climbed to 1,000 feet when he felt a sharp jolt. His plane seemed to stagger in the air. German *ack-ack* had found it. The rotary engine sputtered, roared fitfully for a moment, and then died. Without the noise of the motor, he was uncomfortably aware of the *zip, zip* of the bullets which the anti-aircraft gunners were sending in his direction.

The Camel nosed over in a slow spin. Dave kicked hard on the rudder and pushed the stick forward. As his downward speed increased, he frantically worked the fuel pump, trying to get the engine started again. The Camel was dropping like a rock.

At last some gasoline reached the starving cylinders. The engine sputtered and popped. There was just enough power to pull the plane out of the spin. The nose of the ship lifted toward the horizon, its wheels barely clearing the tree tops.

Gradually the engine lost its roughness. Dave opened the throttle and headed for the nearest cloud bank, tracers followed him as he sped along. Soon a thick layer of clouds hid him from the gunners.

As he turned his ship toward home, another Camel appeared beside him. It was one of the ships of his flight looking for him. Together they headed back to France.

As they passed near Ostend on the coast, Dave saw a Rumpler far below him. Here was his chance to make up for the bad time the Germans had given him. His Camel was damaged, but he couldn't resist the temptation to roll her over and dive down on the Rumpler.

He took the enemy by surprise. With guns blazing away he was on the Rumpler's tail, forcing it into a steep dive. Dave followed until the Rumpler burst into flames and fell into the sea.

It had been quite a day for the young American flier. What had happened to him was the sort of thing he and his friends had discussed in awed tones in the days of the Yale Aero Club. Though he had come close to death, Ingalls was eager to continue with the 213th. No more big, lumbering flying boats for him, even though they might be a great deal safer.

No. 213 Squadron kept him busy. He led his flight in search of German observation balloons, and shot down one himself. Sometimes he and his men escorted British bombers on raids over enemy territory. On these bombing raids it was the job of the Camels to protect the heavily laden bombers from the German fighters that were waiting to pounce. The big bombers

The single-seater Fokker D.VI Scout was introduced late in the war.

were slow and no match for the diving Fokkers. The Camels flew above and on each side of the bombers, constantly on the alert. Sometimes their presence was enough to keep the Fokkers away; sometimes they had to fight them off.

On September 20, 1918, Dave's Camels escorted a flight of bombers deep into enemy territory. There was no trouble until four Fokkers flew out of a cloud. But instead of attacking, the Fokkers seemed to hang back as if waiting for a straggler. A plane that dropped behind was always an easy target.

The Camels could not desert their bombers to drive

off the German planes. On escort duty their orders were to remain with the flight. Instead, the Camel pilots flew along, keeping one eye on the bombers below them and another on the four planes to their left. Suddenly the leader of the Fokker flight swung out and headed for the English planes.

With Dave in the lead, the Camels set off to meet the Germans. The pilot of the first Fokker used the old trick of flying head-on, hoping to force Dave to turn aside. Dave refused to turn and the two ships almost collided before they both broke away. After firing a few shots, the Fokkers withdrew to follow the English planes at a distance.

The Camels had to let them go; they could not leave the bombers unprotected. There might be more Fokkers waiting for just such a thing to happen.

The bombers reached their target and dropped their bombs. As they turned and started for home, one of them was hit by fire from the ground. It continued to fly, but it could no longer keep its place in the formation.

This was what the hovering Fokkers had been waiting for. Two of them swooped on the wounded plane like vultures. But the gunner in the rear cockpit of the damaged bomber was a sharpshooter. He pointed his twin Lewis guns at the attacking planes and held them off.

By this time Ingalls had dropped down to help the bomber. He came up on the Fokkers from the

David Ingalls photographed after the war while he was serving as Assistant Secretary of the Navy.

rear. Because the enemy pilots were concentrating on the crippled bomber, he was able to come in close before he fired. His first blast sent one of the Fokkers spiraling earthward.

Quickly he directed his guns at the remaining Fokker. This time he missed. The Fokker pilot went into a half-roll and then put his ship into a tight spin and disappeared.

The damaged bomber was still staggering toward home. Dave flew along behind it on the lookout for a renewed attack. Three more Fokkers appeared and started to snipe, but they didn't come in close enough for Dave to use his guns effectively. Since he couldn't leave the bomber to chase the Fokkers, he fought a rear-guard action until they reached the safety of the English lines.

In October, 1918, shortly before the end of the war, Dave left the 213th to return to duty with the United States Navy. Before leaving he knocked down another plane, his fifth victory in combat.

For his aid in destroying enemy planes, balloons, and airfields, the grateful British government gave him its Distinguished Flying Cross. The French made him a member of their Legion of Honor. The United States Navy, proud of its only ace, awarded him a Distinguished Service Medal for his "brilliant and courageous" work with No. 213 Squadron.

EDDIE RICKENBACKER THROWS HIS HAT INTO THE RING

The United States was a busy place in the spring and summer of 1917, for the country was preparing to go to war. The Allies, their own armies weakened by almost three years of fighting, asked that American soldiers and sailors be sent to France as soon as possible. They also asked the United States for supplies and financial assistance.

Plans were quickly made to draft a million Americans into the Army. Once in the Army, the men had to be housed, fed, clothed, trained, and then shipped to France with their equipment. The rapidly expanding Army enlarged its standing divisions, at the same time establishing new ones such as chemical warfare. One of the biggest expansions took place in the Signal Corps, whose Aviation Section was responsible for United States military aviation.

The Allies were expecting help from the United

States in the air as well as on the ground. Premier Alexandre Ribot of France asked that an American flying corps of 5,000 pilots, 50,000 mechanics, and 4,500 planes be sent to Europe before the end of 1918 to "enable the Allies to win the supremacy of the air." For an air force that in April, 1917, had only 131 officers, 1,087 enlisted men, and 250 planes— most of them trainers—the French Premier's request was a large order. But an eager group of air officers quickly prepared a plan for an enlarged Aviation Section that would eventually have 22,625 planes. The commander of the Signal Corps, Brigadier General George O. Squier, asked his countrymen to "put Yankee punch into the war by building an army in the air, regiments and brigades of winged cavalry on gas-driven flying horses."

His request met with an enthusiastic response. Americans liked the idea of sending a powerful aerial armada to turn the tide of battle in Europe. Congress appropriated 640 million dollars to finance the expansion program, and planes were ordered from both United States and European companies. Meanwhile the Aviation Section began to train pilots and to organize them into combat squadrons.

One day a young man visited the Signal Corps' Washington headquarters with an idea for a special combat squadron made up of automobile racing drivers and mechanics. He explained that a man who drove a racing car was used to high speeds and his mechanics knew all about engines. Such a squadron would be ready for combat in a very short time. The young man was himself a racing driver, one of the best. His name was Edward V. Rickenbacker.

Rickenbacker outlined his plan for a special squadron to General Squier and several other officers. But he was unable to convince anyone that an automobile racer would make a good aviator.

Next Rickenbacker tried to enlist in the Signal Corps for flight training. He was asked a number of questions about himself, and two of his answers made the recruiting officer shake his head. Eddie was twenty-six, too old for a beginning pilot. And he had left school before finishing the seventh grade. The Signal Corps wanted its pilots to have more education than that.

Rickenbacker was disappointed, but he had learned to make the best of things.

Eddie had grown up in Columbus, Ohio. When he was twelve years old, his father had died. Eddie was forced to leave school to help support his family. He tried a number of jobs—in glass and shoe factories and in a foundry. When he went to work in a garage, he at last found a job he really liked.

That was in 1905 and there weren't many automobiles in Columbus. Most people still depended on horses to take them where they wanted to go. Automobiles were battery-driven, steam-propelled, or powered with a small gasoline engine. All of them were unreliable. Because they broke down so often, Eddie and his employer were kept busy, and Eddie learned a great deal about engines and gears.

Before long the young mechanic decided he wanted to know even more about automobiles than he was able to learn as a helper in a garage. He signed up for a home-study course in automotive engineering. Eddie studied hard every night and at the garage he was able to put to practical use the things he had learned in his lessons. He finished the course in a year's time.

His next job was with the Frayer-Miller Air Cooled Car Company in Columbus. When Frayer-Miller entered one of its cars in the 1906 Vanderbilt Cup Race, Eddie went along to the race as a riding mechanic.

A riding mechanic rode with the driver during an automobile race in order to watch such things as oil pressure and gasoline supply. Unfortunately Rickenbacker's car did not win. A burned-out bearing forced it out of the race, but Eddie acquired a new ambition—to become a racing-car driver.

The young man found the transition from mechanic to driver an easy one. Before long he was racing regularly and winning frequently enough to make a good living. In 1914 he set a new world speed record of 134 miles an hour. By 1917 he had become one of the leading racing-car drivers in the United States.

Early in 1917 Rickenbacker went to England to work on a Sunbeam racing car, which he planned to drive in the automobile races that summer. When it appeared that the United States was going to enter the war, he returned home. Soon afterward he went to Washington with his idea for a special flying squadron of racing drivers.

The Signal Corps didn't want Eddie Rickenbacker, the racing driver, but another branch of the Army did. While he was in Washington, Rickenbacker met General John J. Pershing, commander of the American Expeditionary Forces. The General asked Eddie to enlist and go to France as his staff driver.

Rickenbacker agreed to go with the General. He wasn't especially eager to drive a car in France, but he hoped that once he got there he might be able to arrange a transfer to the Aviation Section. He still wanted to become a pilot.

Rickenbacker drove a staff car for two months. Every time he asked for a transfer to aviation he was told: "You are an excellent driver. As a pilot you may be no good at all. We need you where you are."

One of General Pershing's staff officers was Colonel William Mitchell, soon to become the American air commander in the combat zone. Fortunately for Rickenbacker, Colonel Mitchell liked fast, high-powered cars. One day his big twin-six Packard broke down on

Lieutenant Colonel William Mitchell

the road to Verdun. Rickenbacker, bound for Verdun in a staff car, stopped and offered to help get the Packard started. Colonel Mitchell's driver had worked on the motor for some time and the air officer was impatient at the delay.

When Eddie tried to start the Packard, the engine coughed and died. To the former racing driver's ear, that meant water and dirt in the carburetor. A few minutes later, the carburetor was cleaned out and the car was running again. A pleased and impressed Colonel Mitchell roared off to Verdun.

But the first time Rickenbacker asked Mitchell to help him transfer to the Air Service, the answer was:

"You are too good a driver for that."

Before long Rickenbacker had another opportunity to show Colonel Mitchell what he could do. This time, while he was driving the Colonel to Paris in a Hudson Super-Six, a bearing burned out. Knowing that it would be impossible to obtain another bearing, Rickenbacker found some Babbitt metal and a blow torch. With these he cast a new bearing.

That really impressed Colonel Mitchell. When an engineering officer was needed for the big training base that the Air Service was about to open at Issoudun, he recommended Rickenbacker for the job.

One of the things an engineering officer had to do was to test airplanes after they were repaired. In order to do this testing, Rickenbacker had to learn to fly. In August, 1917, the newly commissioned Air Service second lieutenant began his primary training at a flying school at Tours, France. He had been right in thinking a racing driver would make a good aviator. It took him only seventeen days to win his wings. In September Rickenbacker went to Issoudun, where combat flying was taught. But he had been sent to Issoudun as an engineering officer. Since he was busy all day in the hangars and machine shops, he could practice combat flying only when he had a few minutes to spare. His flight training proceeded slowly.

Nevertheless, Rickenbacker was determined to complete the advanced flight course. Unless he did, he would never get a chance to fly in combat. He

Inspection of planes before flight.

listened to what the instructors told the student pilots. Then, when he had time, he went out and "flew" the lesson.

He learned to do a tail spin and to loop. He learned everything that the Issoudun instructors taught about aerial combat. But his big problem was to arrange a transfer to a combat unit. Unfortunately Rickenbacker did things too well. He had been such a good driver that no one wanted him to do anything else. Now he was such a good engineering officer that the commander at Issoudun wouldn't let him go.

"You are too valuable to be spared," the commander told him. "No one else could do as well."

Rickenbacker, however, was sure his assistant would make a good engineering officer. So Eddie became "ill." For two weeks his assistant was in complete charge. The engineering section ran as well as ever. Having proved his point, Rickenbacker was allowed to go to gunnery school. The gunnery course lasted three weeks, and when a pilot had finished it he was ready for action.

Lieutenant Edward V. Rickenbacker reported to the United States Air Services' 94th Aero Squadron on March 4, 1918. The 94th had just arrived at Villeneuve in northeastern France, where there was no longer much military activity. It was a good place for the Americans to get ready for combat.

When Rickenbacker joined the 94th, the squadron had not yet received guns for its Nieuport fighters. The men began their training for combat in unarmed planes. One of the officers helping with the training was Major Raoul Lufbery. The untried pilots of the 94th Aero Squadron listened carefully to everything the famous ace of the Lafayette Escadrille told them about fighting in the air.

Raoul Lufbery took Rickenbacker on his first flight across the lines. Lieutenant Douglas Campbell, another new man, flew the third plane in the practice patrol. This was the first flight ever made over enemy lines by an American air unit.

The two new pilots tried to appear nonchalant during take-off, but both were nervous and afraid.

Rickenbacker became more so when he discovered his Nieuport could not keep up with the other two. Lufbery, however, circled occasionally to keep his pupil from dropping too far behind.

Rickenbacker found the trenches and shell holes of the lines an appalling sight. No tree or any other sign of life remained. To add to his uneasiness, his plane was rocking in a stiff wind and he began to feel airsick. If he succumbed to airsickness on his first flight over the lines, he would be the laughingstock of the 94th Aero Squadron. The unhappy pilot set his teeth and flew on—into a barrage of anti-aircraft fire.

Shells bursting near the Nieuport caused its rocking to increase. They also made Rickenbacker forget about his airsickness. He had been briefed on the anti-aircraft battery before take-off, and the guns appeared to be every bit as accurate as the reports indicated.

At this point Lufbery turned back to fly alongside Rickenbacker. The presence of the famous ace restored some of Rickenbacker's confidence, and soon he was able to follow Lufbery's maneuvers as they flew beyond the range of the guns and headed for home.

Rickenbacker had survived the ordeal of his first flight over the lines, and he would never be afraid again. He later described that victory over fear as one of the most precious memories of his life.

When they were back on the ground, Lufbery asked both Rickenbacker and Campbell what they had seen during the practice patrol.

"There wasn't another plane in the sky," they said.

That answer amused Lufbery. It was just what he had expected. He proceeded to tell them what they should have seen.

"A formation of five Spads passed under us before we left our lines. Another five Spads went by about fifteen minutes later. They were only 500 yards away. It's just as well they weren't German planes.

"When we turned back there were four German Albatros two miles ahead of us and there was an enemy two-seater nearer than that, at about 5,000 feet above the lines."

Lufbery was teaching the two new pilots how important it was to see everything that moved in the air. It might save their lives one day.

Then Lufbery examined Rickenbacker's Nieuport. In the excitement of flying through the anti-aircraft barrage, Rickenbacker hadn't noticed that his plane had been hit. Lufbery found a shrapnel hole in the tail and another in the outer edge of the wing. A third fragment had passed through both wings barely missing the pilot's seat. Rickenbacker's friends told him afterward that he turned pale and stayed that way for a good thirty minutes.

Early in April the long-awaited machine guns arrived, and were quickly installed on the Nieuports. The 94th Aero Squadron of the United States Air Service became the first American air unit ready for action against Germany.

Although the 94th was ready for action, it had no insignia. After the famous French *Cigognes* squadrons made their stork insignia famous, every combat squadron wanted a distinctive marking for its planes. Someone proposed that the 94th use Uncle Sam's stovepipe hat. Someone else suggested that the hat be painted inside a ring. Throwing a hat into a ring was an invitation to fight. The 94th became the Hat-in-the-Ring Squadron.

The Hat-in-the-Ring Squadron, which had moved to an airfield at Toul, did its first actual fighting on April 14. That day its pilots shot down two German planes. The third victory came two weeks later, on April 29, and was credited to Captain James Norman Hall, who had flown with the *Escadrille Lafayette,* and Lieutenant Eddie Rickenbacker.

The two airmen had been on alert all day. At 5:00 P.M. an enemy ship was reported heading for Toul. Within minutes Hall and Rickenbacker were on their way to intercept it. The excited Rickenbacker saw a plane off in the distance on the right and signaled to Hall. But Hall flew steadily onward. Rickenbacker signaled again. Then, fearful that the quarry would get away, he went after it.

When he got closer, he saw that the plane was a large three-seater. Rickenbacker maneuvered until he came up under its tail. Then, as he lined the plane up in his gun sight, he noticed the markings on its wing—not the black cross of Germany, but the tri-colored circle of France.

Rickenbacker was so embarrassed he could find little satisfaction in the fact that his stalking of the three-seater had been undetected by its occupants. He quickly turned away and flew back to look for Hall.

The chastened Rickenbacker caught up with Hall above the German lines, and this time he followed the more experienced airman. They soon spotted the enemy plane and climbed into the sun, being careful to keep between it and the enemy. Their diving attack took the German pilot by surprise. Even though his Pfalz fighter was a better plane in some respects than the Nieuport, he was unable to get away.

Hall fired first. When the Pfalz responded by heading down toward the German lines, Rickenbacker followed it. At 150 yards he pressed his triggers, directing a stream of bullets along the length of the enemy ship. As the American pulled up, he saw the Pfalz crash to the ground. Rickenbacker and Hall returned to their airfield to find that French observers had already telephoned a confirmation of the victory.

Rickenbacker's next confirmed victory came on May 17 when he shot down an Albatros during an early morning patrol. The future ace had flown above the lines for an hour without seeing an enemy plane. Rather than return to Toul empty-handed, he decided to move farther behind the German lines. He was above an airfield at Thiaucourt, twenty-five miles

Eddie Rickenbacker standing by his Spad. The Hat-in-the-Ring insignia is painted on the fuselage.

behind the lines, when he saw three enemy planes take off and head south. Pleased at the chance for action, Rickenbacker put his Nieuport into a dive that reached 200 miles per hour. When he was fifty yards from the rear Albatros, he fired. It went down.

When the victorious pilot pulled back on his stick for a sharp climb away from the two remaining Albatros, he heard a ripping crash. The canvas of the Nieuport's top right wing tore completely off and the plane turned over on its right side. In his determination to get the Albatros, Rickenbacker had made too steep a dive for a Nieuport. Now he was following the Albatros down.

After spinning to within 3,000 feet of the ground, Rickenbacker opened the throttle, and the resulting burst of speed from the engine leveled the Nieuport. Then he pushed forward on the stick, reversed the rudder, and limped off toward the lines and home.

Enemy anti-aircraft fire gave him a few bad moments over the lines. The damage to his plane prevented his doing anything except fly straight ahead. But he got through the barrage and made a pancake landing at the 94th's field. Rickenbacker climbed from the cockpit unhurt. His victory was confirmed the next day.

Because he was one of the most experienced of the new men in the 94th, Rickenbacker was made a flight commander. But he knew he still had a great deal to learn about aerial combat. He sometimes failed to see

German ships. He didn't always make the right moves in engaging the enemy. He forgot to look behind him. After he became leader of Flight One, he resolved to work harder than ever to improve his own aerial fighting. He would make Flight One the best in the Hat-in-the-Ring Squadron.

Unfortunately Rickenbacker could do little about the Nieuport 28 that the Americans were using. When the United States entered the war, almost all its aircraft were trainers. Not one of them was suitable for combat. To take part in the fighting, American pilots had to use French or British planes—at least until the United States could produce some combat aircraft of its own.

When the 94th moved to the front, the only plane available for the Americans was the Nieuport 28. The Nieuport, however, was no longer the best plane in the air. It had been replaced in French and British squadrons by better fighters.

In the spring of 1918, the Germans began to use the Fokker D. VII, the best of all the fighters produced in Germany during the war. The Nieuports of the 94th were no match for the speedy, maneuverable D. VII, which was a wonderful diver. If the Nieuport was put into a steep dive, it was apt to lose its wings, as Rickenbacker and several other American pilots discovered.

Although Rickenbacker could do nothing about the plane in which he flew, he could do something about the way he flew it. He learned to plan his combat moves carefully. He never refused a fight, but he did try to give himself every advantage over the enemy. He studied his Nieuport as carefully as he had once studied his racing cars. He knew just what he could expect from it.

During a patrol on May 30, 1918, a month and a day after his first victory in combat, the ever-watchful Eddie Rickenbacker saw two Albatros fighters attack a 94th ship. He immediately flew to the rescue, and in the ensuing battle sent one Albatros crashing to earth. When his victory was confirmed several days later, Rickenbacker became an ace.

Officially he was not the 94th Aero Squadron's first ace, however. On May 31 Douglas Campbell shot down a plane, his fifth, and the victory was confirmed at once. To further complicate the matter, Rickenbacker had shot down a plane on May 7, 1918, which was not officially credited to him until January 20, 1960. So the plane he shot down on May 30 was actually his sixth combat victory.

Not long after he became an ace, Rickenbacker developed a serious ear infection. He was sent to a hospital in Paris for a mastoid operation, which kept him from flying for several weeks. When he finally returned to the Hat-in-the-Ring Squadron, then operating from an airfield at Saints in the Chateau-Thierry area, the old Nieuports had been replaced by new Spads.

America's ace of aces, Eddie Rickenbacker, with his favorite Spad scout.

At Chateau-Thierry, American ground troops and air units were helping the French stop a German advance that had driven deep into the Allied lines. Fierce battles raged for several weeks—in the air as well as on the ground. In spite of its new Spads, however, the 94th Aero Squadron did not do too well during its stay at Chateau-Thierry. The Germans were using with great success von Richthofen's flying circus idea. The formations of Fokkers that roamed over the lines shot down several Hat-in-the-Ring pilots.

In addition to being outnumbered in the air, the Americans suffered, first from the inferiority of their

Nieuports, and then from "bugs" in the new Spads. Nevertheless, they received combat experience which prepared them for the next Allied campaign at St. Mihiel.

At St. Mihiel the Allies had planned a surprise attack to wipe out a German-held sector that had extended into the French lines since 1914. American and French air and ground units moved into the area with the greatest secrecy. When the 94th Aero Squadron arrived at its new base at Rembercourt early in September, the men were allowed to use candles at night only if the light could not be seen outside their tents.

After the attack began on September 12, the 94th flew patrols over enemy territory. The squadron was part of a huge force of 1,500 Allied reconnaissance, bombing, and fighter planes under the command of General William Mitchell. Partially because of their superiority in the air, the Allies scored a decisive victory at St. Mihiel in just four days of fighting.

Eddie Rickenbacker downed two German planes during the St. Mihiel campaign. Then on September 25 he received what he has described as "the greatest honor that has ever come to any pilot—the command of the squadron he truly believes the finest in the whole world."

The 94th had been the first American squadron to go into action. The new commander resolved to make it the first American squadron in victories as well. He called his pilots together and explained just what he expected of them. He also told them the most important thing he had learned as a racing driver. "Take care of your engines," he said. "Study them until you know just how much they can do and don't stop short of that point."

The 27th Aero Squadron had been the high scorer among American units at the front, but a week after Rickenbacker took over the 94th his squadron surpassed the 27th. Eddie himself shot down three planes that week, two of them on the twenty-fifth, his first day as commander.

He had taken off on a lone, voluntary patrol that morning. At 13,500 feet he saw twelve Fokkers far off to the east. He was headed in that direction when exploding anti-aircraft shells from an American battery directed his attention to five much closer Fokkers that were escorting two reconnaissance planes. With his back to the sun, Rickenbacker dived on the nearest Fokker and sent it down out of control. Before the remaining Fokkers could reform for a counterattack, Rickenbacker directed his fire at the observation ships and sent one of them down in flames. Twelve years later the American ace was awarded the Medal of Honor for his single-handed attack on the seven enemy ships and his skill in shooting down two of them.

After he became commander of the 94th Aero Squadron, Rickenbacker flew more often than ever.

Rickenbacker proudly displays his Medal of Honor, the highest American military award.

He had decided he would never send a pilot on a mission that he wouldn't undertake himself. He intended to be a commander in the air as well as on the ground. His men were solidly behind their new leader. One of them wrote: "As for Rick, he has a heart of gold and is as square as they make them. Everyone in the squadron is true blue and loyal to him . . . Rick's whole heart is in the 94th Squadron."

In September, 1918, the Allies were advancing almost everywhere on the Western Front. After their success at St. Mihiel, American troops were moved to the Meuse–Argonne sector in eastern France. United States air units also shifted their operations to that area. The airplane had become so important in deciding the outcome of a battle that no commander would order an attack unless he had hundreds of planes at the front.

The attack in the Meuse–Argonne region began on September 26 and was part of the last big Allied campaign of the war. Ordered to eliminate German observations balloons in the area, the members of the Hat-in-the-Ring Squadron also managed to shoot down several enemy planes during the opening days of the offensive. They had other duties as well. One night Captain Rickenbacker and two of his men made a hazardous flight over German territory to check on a report that eleven troop trains were rushing enemy reinforcements to the battle area. The report proved false.

An even more dangerous assignment was the order to make low-level patrols over the battlelines. The pilots of the 94th had to stay below 2,000 feet to drive off the low-flying enemy observation planes that were slipping across the lines. At that height the Americans were within easy range of enemy anti-aircraft fire.

In spite of the dangerous work they did, the 94th lost only five planes during the crucial month of October. They scored thirty-nine victories over the enemy, and their commander, Captain Eddie Rick-

enbacker, raised his own victory score to twenty-six.

Under his leadership the Hat-in-the-Ring Squadron had become an aerial combat unit equal to the best fighter squadrons of France, Britain, or Germany. It was America's answer to the Allies' request for a "flying corps" to help them gain supremacy in the air.

By October, 1918, the Allies had achieved supremacy of the ground as well as in the air. A tight blockade kept badly needed supplies from Germany while American men and supplies were arriving in France in ever increasing quantities. The situation looked so bad that on October 3 Germany sent an appeal for an armistice to President Wilson. It was answered on October 23 with a demand for Germany's unconditional surrender.

Meanwhile the fighting continued with the German army in retreat all along the Western Front. On October 5 the British broke through the once-impenetrable Hindenburg Line and the pressure on Germany increased. In the south her partners, Turkey and Austria–Hungary, surrendered.

In spite of assurance from their generals, the German people were convinced that the war had been lost. A revolution broke out which forced the Kaiser to abdicate. Then, on November 11, 1918, the new German government accepted the Allies' armistice terms. World War I was over.

In four years of fighting, the airplane had developed from a primitive machine of uncertain usefulness into a deadly weapon that could determine the outcome of a battle. The aces and other aviators of Great Britain, France, Germany, and the United States had pioneered a new kind of warfare in which vital lessons were often learned at the expense of a brave man's life. For it took a brave man to meet the enemy high in the sky with only his own skill and courage to see him through to victory.

Before the conflict ended, the day of the lone aerial fighter was already drawing to a close. Groups of planes, such as Germany's Flying Circus, were replacing the single-ship patrol. But the deeds of the men who fought World War I in the sky will live as long as stories of courage are told.

HIGH-SCORING WORLD WAR I ACES

(The rank given is that held on November 11, 1918, or, in the case of those who died, the highest rank attained.)

BELGIAN ACES

	SCORE
Second Lieutenant Willy Coppens	37
Adjudant Andre de Meulemeester	11
Second Lieutenant Edmund Thieffry	10

BRITISH ACES

Major Edward Mannock	73
Lieutenant Colonel William A. Bishop	72
Lieutenant Colonel Raymond Collishaw	60
Major James T. B. McCudden	57
Captain Anthony W. Beauchamp-Proctor	54
Major Donald R. MacLaren	54
Major William G. Barker	53

Captain Robert A. Little	47
Captain Philip F. Fullard	46
Captain George E. H. McElroy	46
Captain Albert Ball	44
Captain John Gilmore	44
Major Tom F. Hazell	41
Captain J. Ira T. Jones	40

FRENCH ACES

Capitaine René Paul Fonck	75
Capitaine Georges Guynemer	53
Lieutenant Charles Nungesser	45
Capitaine Georges F. Madon	41
Lieutenant Maurice Boyau	35
Lieutenant Michel Coiffard	34
Lieutenant Jean Bourjade	28
Capitaine Armand Pinsard	27
Sous-Lieutenant René Dorme	23
Lieutenant Gabriel Guérin	23
Sous-Lieutenant Claude M. Haegelen	23
Sous-Lieutenant Pierre Marinovitch	22
Capitaine Alfred Heurtaux	21
Capitaine Albert Deullin	20

GERMAN ACES

Rittmeister Manfred von Richthofen	80
Oberleutnant Ernst Udet	62
Oberleutnant Erich Loewenhardt	53
Leutnant Werner Voss	48

Leutnant Fritz Rumey	45
Hauptmann Rudolf Berthold	44
Leutnant Paul Bäumer	43
Leutnant Josef Jacobs	41
Hauptmann Bruno Loerzer	41
Hauptmann Oswald Boelcke	40
Leutnant Franz Büchner	40
Oberleutnant Lothar von Richthofen	40
Leutnant Karl Menckhoff	39
Leutnant Heinrich Gontermann	39
Leutnant Max Müller	36
Leutnant Julius Buckler	35
Leutnant Gustav Dörr	35
Hauptmann Eduard von Schleich	35

UNITED STATES

Captain Edward V. Rickenbacker	26
Second Lieutenant Frank Luke, Jr.	21
Major Raoul Lufbery	17
First Lieutenant George A. Vaughn, Jr.	13
Captain Field E. Kindley	12
First Lieutenant David E. Putnam	12
Captain Elliot W. Springs	12
Major Reed G. Landis	10
Captain Jacques Michael Swaab	10

BIBLIOGRAPHY

Adamson, Hans Christian: *Eddie Rickenbacker*. New York: The Macmillan Company, 1946.

Bacon, W. Stevenson (Editor): *Sky Fighters of World War I*. New York: Fawcett Publications, Inc., 1961.

Barrett, William E.: *The First War Planes*. New York: Fawcett Publications, Inc., 1960.

Bordeaux, Henry: *Georges Guynemer, Knight of the Air*. New Haven, Conn.: Yale University Press, 1918.

Cheesman, E. F. (Editor): *Fighter Aircraft of the 1914–1918 War*. Letchworth, Herts: Harleyford Publications, Ltd., 1960.

Cheesman, E. F. (Editor): *Reconnaissance and Bomber Aircraft of the 1914–1918 War*. Los Angeles: Aero Publishers, Inc., 1962.

Cross, Roy: *The Fighter Aircraft Pocketbook*. New York: Sports Car Press, 1962.

Goldberg, Alfred (Editor): *A History of the United States Air Force*. Princeton, N.J.: D. Van Nostrand Company, 1957.

Gray, Peter, and Thetford, Owen: *German Aircraft of the First World War*. London: Putnam, 1962.

Green, William, and Fricker, John: *The Air Forces of the World*. New York: Hanover House, 1958.

Gribble, Leonard R.: *Heroes of the Fighting R.A.F.* London: George G. Harrap and Company, Ltd., 1941.

Gurney, Gene: *Five Down and Glory*. New York: G. P. Putnam's Sons, 1958. Paperback edition: Ballantine Books, Inc.

Mason, Herbert Molloy, Jr.: *The Lafayette Escadrille*. New York: Random House, 1964.

Paine, Ralph D.: *The First Yale Unit*. Cambridge, Mass.: Riverside Press, 1925.

Parsons, Edwin C.: *I Flew with the Lafayette Escadrille*. Indianapolis: E. C. Seale and Company, Inc., 1963.

Reynolds, Quentin: *They Fought for the Sky*. New York: Holt, Rinehart and Winston, Inc., 1957.

Rickenbacker, Edward: *Fighting the Flying Circus*. New York: Frederick A. Stokes Company, Publishers, 1919.

Robertson, Bruce (Editor): *Air Aces of the 1914–1918 War*. Letchworth, Herts: Harleyford Publications, Ltd., 1959.

Robertson, Bruce (Editor): *Von Richthofen and the Flying Circus*. Letchworth, Herts: Harleyford Publications, Ltd., 1958.

Whitehouse, Arch: *The Years of the Sky Kings.* Garden City: Doubleday and Company, Inc., 1959.

Wynne, H. Hugh: "Escadrille Lafayette," in *Cross and Cockade Journal,* vol. 2, no. 1, 1961. (Published by the Society of World War I Aero Historians)

INDEX

ABOUT THE AUTHOR

Gene Gurney was born in Fremont, Ohio. He attended high school in Toledo and is a graduate of the University of Maryland. An Air Force pilot for 19 years, he flew B-24s during World War II and was the first Strategic Air Command combat crew member to fly the KC-135 jet tanker. After the war, he was an Air Force Counter-Intelligence Corps Special Agent, investigating espionage, sabotage, and gold smuggling in the Near East. Lieutenant Colonel Gurney is presently Senior Service representative for the U.S. Air Force in the consolidated Magazine and Book Branch of the Directorate for Information Services, Office of the Assistant Secretary of Defense for Public Affairs.

The author of another popular Landmark Book, *Americans into Orbit,* Gene Gurney has also written several adult books about aviation, including *Five Down and Glory, Journey of the Giants,* and *The War in the Air.* He lives in Prince Frederick, Maryland.

World Landmark Books

U.S. LANDMARK BOOKS